MISCHIEVOUS

Ghost Stories & Illustrations

from the haunted mind of

ADAM D. TILLERY

First Edition:
First printing

PUBLISHED BY HAUNTED ROAD MEDIA, LLC
www.hauntedroadmedia.com

United States of America

For Aunt Jeanie, who enjoyed our ghost stories and encouraged my brothers and me to write more.

ACKNOWLEDGMENTS

I would like to thank everyone who helped me create this book:

Mike Ricksecker, thank you for giving me the chance to create this book and for giving the best writing advice to a nervous investigator at his first paranormal convention, four years ago.

Hannah, I wrote a book! Thank you for your patience and understanding.

To my parents and brothers who helped me remember the stories from long ago. Thank you, Arik and Alec, for sharing your stories and for the good times scaring each other while growing up. Mom and Dad, thank you for reading over my work and for always being willing to help me in any way you can, I am truly grateful. I love you all.

TABLE OF CONTENTS

INTRODUCTION

Long before I knew I was going to explore haunted places for ghosts I enjoyed ghost stories. Tales about ghosts lurking in the shadows or seen floating around old places captivated me.

My interest in ghosts started in the home in which I grew up. It was occupied by more than just my family and me. Ghostly activity took place in my old home, even before I was born. Fortunately, I do not recall any of these spirits to be negative entities of any kind. There would be noises that were unnatural to the home's usual sounds. Footsteps in the attic could be heard and phantom pipe smoke wafting around from the previous owner was unmistakable. He had passed away long ago, but did want to be forgotten. There was even the appearance of a mysterious man dressed in a nice suit, who was seen by my brother, Alec, when he was a child. Twenty years later, my nephew, Caleb, saw and pointed to a man passing through a doorway. He was only two years old when this took place. Caleb uttered the word, "Man."

These are only a few haunting occurrences that contributed to my fascination for ghosts. I was scared at first, but after experiencing so many strange and unexplainable events at an early age, I became quite tolerant of mischievous ghostly behavior.

My curiosity of ghosts has carried into my young adulthood. For the past seven years, I, along with my brother, Alec, and good friend, Gideon Coyle, have been investigating places known for haunting activity as the C.R.E.E.P.Z. Ghost Commandos. I have traveled to the cheeriest cemeteries and to the gloomiest dungeons. I have heard disembodied voices in empty rooms and I have seen shadows creep from the darkness. I have felt the dread of death and the warmth of the afterlife. I have experienced many different hauntings, from the time I began remembering events as a child, to this very moment.

My encounters with paranormal occurrences have filled my head with so many stories, but these stories always began with a vision. When I started exploring haunted locations, images of ghosts manifested in my mind. Being a lifelong artist, I decided to start drawing the visions of these ghosts, and then, write the stories to go with them. The result would be both delightful and terrifying.

The narratives, accounts, stories, poems, and illustrations in this book are a collection of those very ghosts haunting my mind. Some of these ghosts come to me in dreams and some have been shared with me. Others have been inspired by locations I have been to or have personally witnessed.

MY HAUNTED HOME

Collected within this chapter are stories about the haunted house in which I grew up.

My First Ghost Story

July 13, 2015 had already been a strange day. It started with the ambulance being called to my work, which rarely happens, because a girl working in the back had suffered an anxiety attack. She ended up being okay. I had breakfast at my parents' for dinner. I called my girlfriend later and asked what she was having for dinner. Coincidently, she was also having breakfast for dinner, as well. My neighbors, a few houses down, were outside arguing loudly with one another. It has been a fairly quiet neighborhood ever since I moved in several years ago and it was bizarre to hear such loud cussing from six houses down. My girlfriend, who lived a block away could also hear the fight. It had been extremely hot that day as well. Maybe that contributed to the strangeness that had been occurring. However, these events were not the weirdest thing to have happened that day. The most peculiar things happened when I visited my parents after work for dinner.

The previous week I had received the go ahead from the publisher to write this book. I could not contain my excitement any longer and this particular day felt like a good day to tell my parents that I was writing a book! They were very happy and excited for me. I spent many of my school years revising papers that my parents looked over, so I jokingly told them that I was going to need some proofreading done. They laughed but still gladly offered any help.

My parents asked what the title of the book was going to be. I told them that I actually came up with the title while working around their house.

We were uncovering my parent's pool one day and the work was making me thirsty. As I was taking a water break from scrubbing tarp covers, I noticed something as I looked up to take a drink. In attic window I saw a face looking out. It was completely white and bald; I could see its mouth, nose, and eyes gazing out over the neighborhood. However, upon further inspection, I noticed that it was just a mannequin head. I laughed and pointed it out to my older brother, Alec. He laughed, too, and asked me if I was just now noticing it. He went on to say it was either put up there by mom or our older brother, Arik. We agreed it was most likely our oldest sibling.

"How mischievous of him," I thought.

Then it hit me, "Mischievous!"

I had been contemplating the title of the book while I was writing various ghost stories, and "Mischievous" seemed to pretty much describe a good chunk of my stories.

My parents laughed after I told them how I came up with the title. They were, also, aware of the mannequin head and assumed it was Arik's doing as well. After discussing a little more about what was going into my book, my dad motioned to an old picture placed on a shelf in the kitchen. It was a picture of my Grandpa on my mom's side.

"He was mischievous too," said my dad.

My mom smiled and told me a story about Grandpa being mischievous:

"When my brothers and I were really young we would often play in the backyard. One night we heard a commotion in the garage. My brothers and I went to the side door to see if the loud noises were coming from there. We peaked inside and became frightened when we saw objects flying across the garage. My brothers and I ran straight back to the house to find our parents. We made it to the back door. The door would not open. We were terrified of whatever may be in the garage, tearfully and desperate we tried to get inside the house, but the door still would not open. While we shouted and yelled for the door to open, your Grandma and Grandpa were laughing away on the other side. Your Grandpa had been hiding in the garage when my brothers and I came to check out what the noises were. He had moved something, and hooted like an owl while hidden away in the darkness. When my brothers and I darted back to the house your Grandpa ran quickly around the other side of the garage, then around the house. He entered through the front door of his house where he found your Grandma holding the door shut."

Grandpa was indeed mischievous. It was the first time I'd heard that story and it just makes me smile knowing that same playfulness still runs in the family.

My parents and I talked a little further about some of the stories that were going to be in the book. My mom told me she had a ghost story of her own. I asked her if it was the one that happened before I was born. It was, in fact, but I wanted to hear it again. I'd heard it when I was younger and didn't remember many the details. With ghost stories becoming a growing passion of mine, I had to know details and remember it properly. My mom obliged and began the story, as she remembered:

"You were just a baby in my tummy when I was upstairs in the rocking chair holding Alec. It was nearly midnight as I unwound from such a sad day of attending your Grandpa's funeral. I sat in the chair trying to shake my concerns away when something in

the backyard caught my attention. It was dark and a storm was forecasted. Lightning flashed above the clouds. Suddenly, I could see someone standing in the backyard between the big oak tree and the swing set. It was a man in a white suit standing and looking at me with an eased expression on his face. I didn't feel threatened; in fact, I felt calm. The man's image only lasted a few seconds but I could just make out who it was. The white suit was familiar to me because it was the same suit your Grandpa was wearing at his funeral. A clock chimed when midnight came. I gave the clock a quick glance and when I turned to look back outside your Grandpa was gone. His appearance comforted me. His relaxed expression and the calm I felt when I saw him made me feel some comfort and a sense that he was just coming one last time to say goodbye."

That was it, my first ghost story and I only was on my way to being born nine months later. After she had told me the story another one of those strange things happened that had been occurring throughout the day.

When my mom ended the story I was wondering upon what day that had happened. Before I could ask her she continued, "Your Grandpa passed away 33 years ago today, and his funeral was three days later."

I was stunned! Of all the days I tell my parents that I'm writing my first book about ghost stories I hear *this* ghost story from my mom on the anniversary of my Grandpa's passing. I had chills unlike any I'd ever had.

Sometimes the signs telling that you are on the path you are supposed to be are strangely all around you. Coincidences, flukes, or an odd quirk? I do not know. So when I am in doubt, I'll go with what I do know. It is that July 13, 2015 was way out of the ordinary for me not to take notice of the strange occurrences and coincidences happening throughout the day. I can't help but think that my first ghost story and this book are connected in some extraordinary supernatural way.

Our Haunted House

I have so many memories of playing games with my brothers, dad working outside, mom cooking in the kitchen, and the ghosts, with whom we shared our home. I can still feel every edge of the house on my fingertips. I am thankful I became mature enough in time to appreciate the last few years in that house. During that time I often reflected on every memory that came to my mind. Those reflections made me realize that the house itself was like a family member that I never fully appreciated. It sheltered, comforted, and entertained me just as much as a person would have. I exerted so many emotions and memories there that a part of me feels like it was left behind. I would like to go see it again but there is no need. It would be like trying to recover something I never lost and I would only be chasing memories I already have. Sometimes I wonder if thoughts like these are the same thoughts that make a ghost come back to visit a place that was once theirs.

The house where I grew up was in the Woodcrest neighborhood of Kansas City, Kansas. It helped me gain an understanding of the word "haunted." I cannot say for sure that I have seen a ghost in the house but all of my other senses knew they were there. The house seemed to purposely make eerie knocks and whispers to get our attention. My parents and brothers also knew that we were not alone in the house. Even our pet cats, Cinnamon and Pepper, would sometimes weird us out when they intensely stared at blank walls and corners of rooms where there was nothing of interest to look at. From everyone hearing footsteps pacing in the attic to my oldest brother's imaginary friend named Johnny, we all had a ghostly encounter at some point. Some situations were more frightening than others, but most of the time a ghostly occurrence would not even make us think twice. A good example of this would be the watcher in the basement.

Shortly after my dad and grandpa converted the basement into a library and a recreation room we started seeing and feeling things in the basement that we had not experienced before. One of the common things almost everyone saw was a ghostly figure we called "the watcher."

If you were hanging out in the recreation room, watching TV, or playing video games, at some point you would see someone out of the corner of your eye slowly peeking around the corner. At first you would be scared by the feeling of being watched. A swift glance at the figure staring at you made it vanish very quickly. No matter how often you would get up to see who was around the corner, no one would ever be there. It happened so often that eventually we told it "we see you!" Or we would just ignore it. It never fully came around the corner. All it ever did was watch us, so we thought. There were a few instances where something was seen and felt down in the basement. My cousin, Justin, and my friend, Gideon, both saw a strange red-headed woman in the library quickly disappear around the corner by the stairs leading up to kitchen. Another eerie occurrence happened to my sister-in-law when she felt a hand brushing her hair while she was doing school work on our computer, but those are stories for another time.

Fortunately, there was nothing ever threatening about the spirits. It could be startling but the experiences were never too terrifying to the point of making us want to leave the house.

I can remember when falling asleep at night, I would sometimes hear faint whispering coming from the doorway of my room. I would barely open my eyes and peek over my sheets towards my door to see who it was but there would be no one. Only the voices of a man and woman whispering to one another were heard. I never could understand what they were saying but occasionally I would hear my name. It was definitely spooky to think about it now, but back when it happened I was young and didn't quite understand how to interpret what I was experiencing.

When my brothers and I were younger, our parents explained to us that these strange occurrences happening in the house were probably just the former owners or perhaps a passed relative coming by to visit. They explained them to us in a way that made them sound as harmless as Santa Claus or the Easter Bunny. My parents handled the idea of ghosts in the house really well. They didn't deny it, even though my dad was skeptical at times. Their attitude towards ghosts in the house was very casual yet I could see by their slight smiles that they were intrigued by the possibility just as much as we were when my brothers and I would tell them about something spooky happening in the house.

I haven't driven by our old house since we moved out. The irony isn't that I'm afraid of seeing the ghosts. I am afraid to see what has become of the home where I grew up.

Pipe Smoke

One of my earliest memories from our old home was when we would smell the sweet scent of aromatic tobacco pipe smoke drifting around the house. No one in my family had smoked so the smell was always a mystery to me and my brothers as we grew up in the house. The scent could be picked up at various times of the day and night in all different parts of the house but it was heaviest in two particular areas of our home. This smoky smell lingered longest in our living room near one of the front windows and it would hang thickly in the basement where an old coal room used to be. My brothers would come across it so often that we asked our parents if they were burning something in the house. They never were burning anything unless it was a flowery scented candle or some of mom's good cooking which was nothing like tobacco smoke. However, our parents knew the pipe smoke scent quite well. They had noticed it years ago when they met the original owners of the house.

My parents visited the former owners back in the 1970s. They told us that they were an elderly couple and were very nice. They were the original owners of the home and had been living there since it was built in the late 1920s. I don't remember my parents telling me too much about them other than they had a daughter, but she had moved away long ago. Another interesting thing my parents told us was how there used to be brown paper covering the windows and strings all around the house. Mrs. Harris used the strings to find her way around the home because she was sensitive to light and nearly blind.

However, the most intriguing story they told us was about how Mr. Harris smoked a pipe. He enjoyed smoking his pipe in the living room and looking out the front window. When his wife didn't want him to smoke upstairs he would go down into the basement to smoke his pipe in the old coal room. It just so happens, these two areas are where the pipe smoke was smelled the most!

Now, could it just be the old smoke seeping from the walls and the carpet? Maybe, but the pipe smoke lingers, as fresh and sweet, as the day it was puffed. Also, my parents moved into the house in the mid-1970s and the old carpets have been removed and replaced, and the walls and ceilings have had several coats of paint, since.

It wasn't until a few years ago that I decided to look up Mr. and Mrs. Harris to see what became of them. Being an investigator of ghosts, I wanted to find some validity to the haunting occurrences in our home. Indeed, if this was, Mr. Harris' spirit coming back to his former home to enjoy a few puffs of his pipe, then he would have to have died before 1983, the year I was born, or before I could start remembering the phantom pipe smoke for myself. Eventually, I was able to find the Harris' gravesites on the internet. A photo of Mr. Harris' gravestone came up; it read that he passed away 1982, a year before I was born.

To my family and me, we knew the recurrent aroma was from a man at peace with his pipe and not to be feared.

Shaken Awake

The time finally came when our old house was ready to be sold. We were still gradually moving things out of the house while the real estate sign was being stuck in the front yard. It was a bittersweet moment but it was time to move on. There only a few neighbors left who were sad to see us go but happy that the neighborly friendship lasted between us for so many years.

Two neighbors in particular, an elderly couple who lived a couple houses up from us and were probably the oldest in the neighborhood, were our dearest neighbor friends. They were there long before my parents moved into the neighborhood. We would visit with each other often through the years. We would always talk about the neighborhood and the comings and goings occurring throughout it.

When the husband passed away, the couple's son came home to live with his mother. Everyone who knew the old man in the neighborhood was saddened at the news of his passing and the neighbors comforted the widow and their son when they could. Frequent calls were made to ask how she was doing. After a few years, she adjusted to life without her husband and her grief had lessened.

When the time came to sell our house it was hard breaking the news to our close neighbors. However, everyone understood and knew that we still would still keep in touch.

The house did its job in helping raise my brothers and me. My parents found a new place with less worries. Our old home needed updates and the crime rate seemed to be closing in on the neighborhood.

Until the house was sold, my parents were very vigilant in keeping it safe. They wanted to make sure no one was breaking in at night while we were away. Motion lights and timers were set up all over the house to deter any would be thieves. My parents concern was so great that sometimes one of them would spend the night alone in the house alone just to keep an eye on things.

By now plenty of ghost stories had been shared by me, my brothers, and my Mom, but it was a rare moment when my dad had one to tell.

One evening dad spent the night in the house. It was an ordinary night and all was house quiet. Dad closed up the house, set up the security, and went upstairs to bed. Most of the night he had slept peacefully.

It was early in the morning and still dark out when my dad suddenly awoke. He thought something had moved in the room but he didn't pay too much attention to the noise. He just shifted around in bed to a comfortable position and soon fell back asleep. A few moments later he was awoken again. This time he looked up from his pillow and peered around the bed. Dad thought he had felt the bed shake! He laid still a while longer before trying to fall back asleep, but then the bed shook again. To him it felt like someone was standing at the edge of his bed shaking it urgently. He quickly sat up to see who or what was shaking the bed but there was no one around and nothing else was moving in the room.

Trying to make sense of the shaking bed he soon noticed something out the bedroom window. Red and blue lights flashed on the side of the neighbor's house. Dad quickly got up and went downstairs to the front room to look out of the window. A firetruck and an ambulance were parked out in front of our neighbor's house which happened to be the widow's house.

Dad quickly dressed and rushed over to their house to see what had happened. He found out that our neighbor's son had gotten up in the middle of the night and accidently fell down a stairway and broke his neck.

Fortunately, the son recovered to the relief of his mother but my dad was left wondering about being awoken in the middle of the night. He seriously thought someone was shaking the bed to wake him up. Dad was never frightened by the experience and tried to think of a logical explanation for the bed shaking but there was none. In all the years that he lived there, the bed he slept in never shook on its own until that night. He couldn't help but wonder, had a supernatural force played a part in his checking up on the neighbor that was in need of his help?

One Last Tour of My Old House

The closing dates were coming up on the old house I grew up in and I wanted to take my girlfriend, Hannah, there before it was sold. I wanted to show her where I grew up, the place that shaped me into the person I am today. She knew I researched ghosts and that the house that we were going to had its share of ghost stories but nothing strange had happened to me in the house for quite some time. Along the way I told her more about growing up at the house, but I didn't elaborate too much, on the ghost stories because I didn't want to scare her away. Little did I know that she was already thinking of the haunting occurrences that could happen to her in the house. I had told her that if she was scared that we didn't have to go, but she was brave at the time and didn't show any hint of fear.

We arrived at the house and began the tour. We entered through the garage but before we did I told her that she may want to plug her ears. The garage door was old, original, and made quite a ruckus when opening and closing it. Hannah laughed at how ridiculously noisy the garage door was but was fascinated at the sight of its age and ability to still function properly. I closed the garage door behind us and we entered through another door that led to the recreation room in the basement. Even after building the recreation room and library we could never fully get rid of the musty old basement smell. I never minded the smell. The scent reminded me of when I was younger and would head to the basement to cool off from a hot summer day with video games or to watch a movie.

After showing her the basement, we made our way up the stairs that led to the kitchen. Through the kitchen was the dining room where the home's original ornate light fixture still hung in an empty room. Beyond the dining room, through a large cherry wood archway, was the living room. The shades were all pulled down except for the ones on the front room windows. The outside light streamed in giving the empty living room and dining room an eerie glow.

I could see the hesitation in Hannah's eyes but she was "hanging in there." I assured her there was nothing to be afraid of in the house. Sure it looked a little spooky without furniture and no lights on but I feel that is normal for any place with similar conditions.

We made our way to the hallway where I stood in the middle of it pointing to the rooms and doors and explained what was in them or behind them. Hannah was feeling a little more comfortable and peered in a few rooms herself. I stopped talking for a bit and in the silence both Hannah and I suddenly jumped when a hissing noise broke the silence. I immediately knew what it was and forgot to warn Hannah what else she might encounter in the house that may startle her. My mom had placed motion activated air fresheners throughout the house to keep it smelling nice for when potential buyers would come to look at the place. The hissing air freshener startled Hannah, making her heart race. She assured me that she was okay. Jokingly, I told her that it was better to experience that than a real ghost in the house. She playfully squinted her eyes and scowled at me as I snickered at her fright.

Next, we went to the pink room at the end of the hallway. It used to be my oldest brother's room, but when he moved out my mom painted the room a tasteful shade of pink and made it a guest bedroom. I was standing in the room and Hannah was standing near the doorway as I explained what the room used to be. I could see that she was still wary of automatic air fresheners which made her cautiously enter rooms. I continued to assure her that there wasn't anything else that was going to scare her. Well, it was not long after I said that when a loud "KNOCK" followed by the fading sound of footsteps walking towards the back house was heard coming from the attic above us. I was quick to calm her by telling her that it could have been just a squirrel running on the roof or something falling from a tree, but she was still on edge.

After showing her the pink room, we went back into the hallway, to the door leading to the second floor where the parents' room and the attic was. Just as I was about to reach for the doorknob to open the door, two knocks came from the other side of it. Hannah was officially freaked out! She'd had enough.

Hannah instantly winced and looked at me if I had done something. However, she quickly realized that the noise had nothing to do with me when she saw that I had become wide eyed and still from hearing the knocking. I remember Hannah throwing her hands up and rushing her way back to the kitchen, down the stairs to the basement, and to the garage where she waited for me to let her out. The unexplained noises coming from the attic and the mysterious knocks on the upstairs door were enough for her and she was ready to go.

I was in a slight disbelief at the familiar noises. It had been a while since I last heard them. I quickly followed behind Hannah to get her outside and make her feel comfortable again. While holding back a smile of amusement I told her how I could not believe that had happened.

Of all the days for something to happen there I am glad it was on that day. Although she was not too thrilled at the time, I am still strangely happy that Hannah had a chance to experience the haunting and mysterious noises of the home in which I grew up. I feel the mischievous actions of a ghost in my old home made her believe that I wasn't all that kooky when I spoke about my ghost stories.

It has been nearly four years since that day we took a tour of my old home. Hannah is better when dealing with my ghost hobbies but she still does not like being in spooky situations. Nevertheless, she still enjoys hearing about the haunted places I have visited. Now when I ask her if she would like to go to these locations, she is quick to remind me of when I took her to the house in which I grew up.

DREAMS & NIGHTMARES

I have vivid dreams and nightmares of ghosts, both good and bad. These are accounts of my most memorable meetings with the supernatural while I slept.

Whirling Winds & Whispers

My room was at the end of the long hallway in the house in which I grew up. My older brother took a room down the hall when my oldest brother moved out. A room all to myself is a young boy's dream. I had my own space to do whatever I wanted, decorate however I wanted, and arrange my furniture wherever I wanted. This was one of my first tastes of independence and expressing myself. The dresser was between the door to my room and the door to my closet, a TV was on top of the dresser, my stereo and CD collection was put next to my desk in one corner of the room, and I pushed my bed to the other corner of the room where the windows were. After putting up a few displayed posters and decoratively positioned toys, the room had become all mine, or so I thought.

I had been settling in nicely to my room. It wasn't that hard to adjust with my brother no longer in the same room, but the room did become more eerie at night knowing that I was all alone with the nearest person being a long sprint down the hall or upstairs to my parents' room. I think the ghosts of the house knew this, too.

Our family always suspected there was a ghost or two in the house. It was normal for us to hear footsteps in the attic or smell the pipe smoke from one of the previous owners. Even my brother, Alec, saw a man looking at him from the hallway when he was child, but that is another story he could tell better. Throughout the years, the usual noises at night of the settling house became stranger and more unusual.

It was in the mid-1990s when my attention to the ghosts in the house began to heighten. The feeling of being watched became more intense and the house activity seemed to pick up, especially when I was home alone. My sleeping habits began to change, too. Right before I was about to fall asleep something in my room would make a noise and jolt me awake. I would wonder if it was something moving or the floor creaking in my room. The noises were always quick and would only happen once or twice a night. I would pop up and look around to see if something had fallen or if someone was in my room. Nothing was ever out of place and no one was ever there. Over time, I became used to the noises and would ignore them. Nothing was ever there, so it no longer worried me. However, I remember one night in particular that has stuck with me and has made a major contribution to my fascination with ghosts.

The night had been normal and I fell asleep quite easily. I planned to sleep in because no was going to be home to wake me up in the morning. My parents were going to run some errands and my brother was heading out to hang with his friends for most of the day. As I slept, I remember waking up in the middle of the night, but I don't think it was a noise that had awoken me.

I went back to sleep and remember that my dreams were strange for the rest of the night. I recall feeling awake, but knew I was dreaming. Then, I remember lying there and opening my eyes, but the room was completely black. No street lights came through my windows and no lights from inside the house glowed into my room. I couldn't even see my digital clock near me which always glowed red with the current time. Even though I couldn't see anything, I felt comfortable.

Suddenly, my body began to float a few inches off of my bed. I heard the wind outside begin to blow. The wind began to pick up and blew all around me, swirling as if I were in a storm. It was becoming so loud and deafening that I began panicking in my dream, thinking it was a tornado from a sudden storm and it was coming right over the house! I dropped back down onto my bed and awoke.

Immediately, I pulled my curtain aside to see to see how bad this storm was. To my astonishment, it was completely calm outside, a quiet overcast day. I remember staring at the bushes outside my window and not seeing a single leaf stir. I laid back down in relief and squinted over to my clock which read 9:00 AM something. It was morning and it had all been a dream.

I laid there awhile, thinking about how the wind sounded so real to me and how bizarre the floating sensation had been. Just as I was about to fall back asleep, I heard something *I knew* was real. I didn't move or open my eyes even though I was quite startled. At my doorway, I heard two people whispering. I was terrified, but my eyes unwilling opened to see who was whispering. I hoped it was my parents or brother, but as I looked through squinted eyes I saw no one and the whispering stopped.

I slowly pulled the covers over my head and didn't move. I laid there for a while longer expecting to hear something move closer to me. I waited and waited, but there was nothing. I was getting comfortable, again, but kept the sheets over my head. The warmth of my bed was making me dose off. As I drifted back to sleep, I heard someone next to my bed whisper, "Adam."

The Long Dark Stairs

When I was growing up in the neighborhood of Woodcrest off N. 40th Street, the yards surrounding my house were the whole world to me. In the front yard I was a star football player throwing amazing touchdown passes to my brothers and neighborhood friends. The side yards were my drag strips for the rickety go carts I would make from my dad's scrap wood pile. During the winter it was the perfect sledding slope after a nice snowfall. My brothers and I channeled a perfect sledding path in the snow that would start from the top of the backyard, passing through the narrow side yard gate, and ending just before the edge of the street at the bottom of the front yard. Mom would often come out to check on us to see if we were attempting to cross the street with our sleds, which she did not approve of. The front yard sloped down to the street with nothing to stop us. We intentionally wiped ourselves out to slow our momentum from heading into the street. The wipeouts were spectacular displays of flailing limbs and rolling bodies. It never hurt us, our bodies were impervious to serious injury thanks to the durable 1980s one-piece snow suits.

Every part of the yard and every tree was a setting for my imagination. My favorite setting, or yard, was in the back: fenced off, tall trees, patio, deck, and our clubhouse. The clubhouse was the epicenter of my outdoor imagination. From atop the clubhouse my brothers and I could see all around the neighborhood, whenever trees and houses permitted. We could even see the movies playing, on a nice fall or winter day when the trees were leafless, at the State Avenue Drive-In which was about a mile away to the southwest. I remember my dad telling me that the top of the backyard was the second highest point in all of Kansas City, Kansas.

The clubhouse was many things to us, but it was mainly our base for our neighborhood club called the "Commandos." It was a hideaway when our shenanigans around the neighborhood got us into trouble, and it was our shelter during summer campouts with our neighborhood friends. Many meetings were held and countless adventures were conspired there.

One adventure our club often talked about was a journey far beyond our neighborhood boundaries. Directly east of the clubhouse, through some neighbors' backyards, across a street called Praun Lane, and over an old fence was a vast rolling field that overlooked a valley of trees. The trees evenly lined the horizon, but there was something that stood out amongst them.

High above the trees an old tower arose. It was a red brick tower with large glassless windows and deteriorated white woodwork framing them. The tower was crowned with a tarnished copper dome and a cross at its pinnacle. Just a few steps north of the clubhouse we could stand on an old rock wall at the edge of the backyard and easily see the tower peering over the trees.

Our parents told us it was a monastery and that monks lived there. This building originally was the Kansas City University built in 1887. As an adult, I see the monastery as a beautiful piece of architectural history, but as a kid it was a source of mystery and spooky ghost stories. We told many stories about ghosts and monsters in our neighborhood, and our favorite time to share them was at night or during a campout. A few of the tales would be about the monastery and they always chilled us the most. The stories usually involved long dead monks wandering around the fields at night holding lanterns looking for something or someone to take back to the monastery for various frightening reasons. I may remember a tale or two, but those are for another time.

Just knowing the monastery with its mysterious monks was just a street and an old fence away, our eyes would begin to play tricks on us as we peeked outside the clubhouse when the wind oddly stirred or when the crack of a twig snapped. Our already terrified minds and sleepy eyes would make us think we saw dark robed figures throughout the shadowy parts of the backyard and in the surrounding neighborhood. We would eventually scare ourselves to sleep as we tried to stay awake and alert in case any ghosts or monsters tried to creep up on us.

Those were some of the most memorable and exciting times of my youth. In fact, those same clubhouse campouts and ghost stories told twenty some years ago are big inspirations for me to write this book! However, they also inspired a nightmare that has haunted me since my childhood. The nightmare was quick, but I remember it vividly, even after all this time. I didn't even have it during a campout or after a night of telling ghost stories or talking about monsters. For this nightmare to stick in my head while others have been forgotten throughout all this time has made me believe it had a certain power connected to it; a power of the paranormal kind.

When the dream began, I had crossed Praun Lane and hopped the fence to the monastery field. Day quickly faded into night and I was now floating toward the monastery. All went black and the next thing I remember was that I was standing at the top of a staircase inside the monastery. It was dark with the only light coming from the windows that face back out across the trees and fields. It was nighttime outside, but a dusky blue-grey color still seeped in. I turned my attention to the stairs that wound down into darkness. Had I been in control of the nightmare, I would not have descended this long and dark staircase, but unwillingly I did.

The stairs were many and its descent was long. Step after step, slowly down the stairs for what seemed like a very long time, the bottom, finally, came into sight. A single light had shone down onto what appeared to be a stone block on black and white checkered tiles, but I do not recall seeing from where the light came. I remained on the stairs before proceeding to the very bottom. The light did not reveal any walls or windows or any other items in the room. Only this large stone block centered below the light and the endless checkered tile floor that faded into darkness.

The block looked damaged on the top, as I cautiously finished descending the staircase and slowly approached it. The stone block was long, but not very wide and stood just a few inches shorter than I. The top of the block became clearer to me the closer I got. I noticed it was not damaged as I thought; instead what I had seen was a lid that sat ajar on top of the stone block. The slightly opened lid revealed that this large stone block was actually hollowed out. I reeled when I made sense of what I was looking at. It was a tomb!

I recoiled and screamed with fright. I carefully stepped backward to the stairs, as my scream echoed and faded into stillness. I expected monks to jump out and grab me, but nothing happened. I made my way to the edge of the stairs when a deep grinding sound pierced the silence. I turned and saw the lid on the tomb slowly opening further. I had no idea what was opening it and I didn't stick around to see what it was.

I dashed up the stairs, as quickly as I could, but it was not fast enough. I could hear something pursuing me up the stairs, and it was gaining on me. I tried to run faster, but, unfortunately being in the world of dreams, my legs felt sluggish, as if I were running in thick swampy mud that tried to pull me under with each step. The clamber of my pursuer drew nearer as I tried in vain to evade whatever it was, but it was too late. I felt the swipe of cold hands trying to clasp me in its grip!

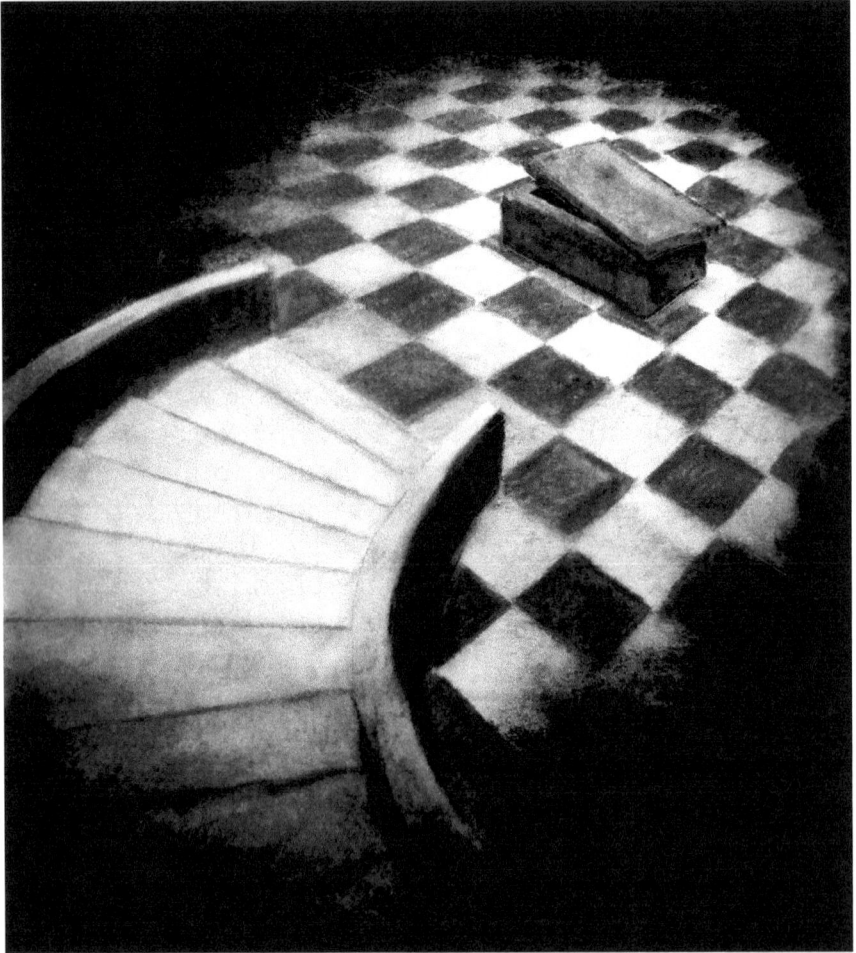

The horrific pursuer had awakened me from my nightmare. I had woke up in a cold sweat and a frightening memory of the monastery that has never faded.

The Numbered

Of this nightmare I can recall only a little, and it turned out to be not as frightening as when it started.

It began in the basement of the old home in which I grew up. At the time, my dad and grandpa were building rooms in the basement. I was standing in the laundry room and could still see out across the basement through the wooden beams that framed the potential rooms.

Suddenly, there were glowing blue apparitions appearing everywhere! They frightened me very much, but they were not all that terrifying to look at. They all had somber faces that looked at the ground or off into some unknown distance. These spirits began to form a single file line and made their way toward me in the back of the laundry room. Their slow, meandering approach made my heart race. They seemed aware of my presence, but weren't bothered by me. I braced myself against the basement freezer, because I had no escape. The line of ghosts stretched across to the other end of the house and far enough away to where I couldn't see from where it was they were coming. They all came to me reverently.

The first spirit to approach me was a lady with her hair pulled into a bun who wore a brown skirt and a tan sweater. I would have guessed her age to be in the late thirties. The lady stopped right in front of me and I, for some unknown reason, uncontrollably began to mark her forehead with a number. She looked directly at me with a cold stare. After writing the number on her forehead she turned to the left, took a step and disappeared into another plane of existence. The next spirit came toward me and I assigned another number to his forehead. This continued on for quite a while, then the dream faded and I gently woke up.

Still, I don't know what to make of this dream even after all these years. Was it just my interest in the home's ghosts being taken to a visual and imaginative extreme? Considering my actions in the dream, I honestly hope it was for that reason.

Attachment

I had just come home from a long ghost investigation at the John Wornall House Museum in Kansas City, Missouri. In 1858, the home began as the residence of the Wornall family, but when the American Civil War forced them from their home, the house was used as a field hospital for both the Union and Confederate soldiers who fought in the Battle of Westport. The John Wornall House Museum was one of my first investigations and I had some truly frightening experiences there. I can say for certain the Wornall House helped develop my early tolerance for fear while exploring places for ghosts.

My brother, Alec, and good friend, Gideon, were trying a new technique at the time which required us to spread out at a location and investigate certain areas alone. I volunteered to go into the kitchen where reports of a child spirit named "Mitty" was said to be frequenting. Without Alec or Gideon nearby the house seemed to close in on me and become more aware of my presence. I began asking the typical questions of a ghost investigation and received the usual eerie answers. A knock here and an unexplained noise there but what I didn't expect was something heard with my ears and not picked up on our recording devices.

I like to give long pauses in between my questions, so there is time for the spirits to answer me. During one of those long pauses, I thought I heard a voice trying to answer one of my questions, but instead sounded like distant crying! The crying only lasted for few a seconds. It chilled me to the bone, and I froze where I stood. I had a voice recorder rolling, but nothing was captured on it. However, the camcorder I was holding did capture the moment and my expression when I heard the crying, but the audio failed to record the disembodied crying sound.

I regrouped with Alec and Gideon and told them of my experience. They didn't recall hearing anyone crying and nothing unusual happened to them. For the rest of night, I was really on edge and was expecting to encounter another ghostly situation around the next corner.

After exploring the main house, we made our way to the old carriage house that is located behind the John Wornall house. The building is primarily used for storage, but what we experienced in there seemed to have more activity than in the Wornall house. We heard stories about people having felt a heavier feeling in the carriage house and some people had even been touched!

One of the stories was about the ghost of a man upstairs in the carriage house who, in life, could have been a slave or an overseer of the property who used to work on the land. When we entered the carriage house, we all felt the heaviness of the building, and we found ourselves sneaking around so as not to disturb the spirit reported to be in there. We composed ourselves and continued conducting our investigation. We were only a few questions into our investigation and we received a response we didn't expect. Earlier in the day, we had performed a basic sweep of the carriage house with our meters to see if there were any odd fluctuations. We did indeed find some odd readings near the center of the carriage house on the main level. When we returned that night, we swept the area, again, with our meters. To our surprise, there were no fluctuations at all on our meters. The strange energies we had picked up earlier were gone.

When we were approaching the stairs to the second floor of the carriage house, we asked questions along the way to try to get a response on our recording devices while looking for strange readings on our meters. Just a few steps from the stairs our meters began to light up. This indicated an electro-magnetic disturbance nearby. As soon as we noticed our meters detecting something, Alec and I heard what sounded like a growl come from upstairs! Shortly after hearing this growl, creaky wood noises were heard coming from the second floor. The sound startled us for a few seconds, and we tried comprehending what we had just heard. Our courage eventually overcame the noise that stunned us, and we gradually made our way upstairs. We cautiously searched around the second floor but did not find out what made the noises, and we didn't encounter any other ghostly activity.

It was an intense investigation and it truly tested our bravery and willingness to explore further. We did come out of it chilled, but we were still thrilled about the events of the night. We were also excited to see what we may have captured on our recording devices. To our amazement, there was the growl on audio after reviewing our devices!

We were tired, but felt good after our investigation. All the way home we discussed our experiences at the John Wornall House Museum and looked forward to the next investigation.

By the time Alec had dropped off Gideon and I weariness was settling in. After unloading Alec's vehicle I left my equipment in the kitchen, kicked off my boots, and headed straight for bed. I crawled under the covers and, again, recounted my experiences during the investigation until I drifted into a deep sleep.

I don't remember dreaming much, but I do remember quite clearly the nightmare I had that night, and I am almost certain it was brought on by my experiences at the John Wornall House Museum. The nightmare, I believe, was an actual case of attachment because the dream's content was truly powerful and relevant for investigation ghost activity.

Within the nightmare I was in a dark basement almost entirely pitch black except for a window in the background that let in a dim purplish light. I was walking toward the window and asking questions along the way then stopped suddenly. A pale hand reached at me from out of the darkness!

I threw up my arm in defense and tried to hit it away, but its fingers with its dark nails grabbed deep into my forearm and began pulling at me. I had never felt more fear in my life! Something intended to harm me and I felt powerless to stop it. Suddenly, I heard a voice in my head telling me say, "Light of God."

Without hesitating in my nightmare I shouted, "Light of God!"

White light filled the room and surrounded me. In an instant, the nightmare was over and I was startled awake. The hand was gone and I felt safe.

I was breathing heavily as I sat up in my bed. The room was already filled with the sun's morning light. I checked my arm and it was fine.

I believe spirits can attach themselves to you and can come home with you after an investigation. Since that nightmare, I take more precautions to avoid bringing home spiritual attachments.

I also feel extremely lucky to have heard that voice speak to me. I feel it was a guardian on the side of good protecting me from a real evil. To this day, whenever I feel threatened while on an investigation, while trying to sleep, or just going about my everyday business, I remember back to that nightmare and repeat the those valuable words I was told to say and the presence of evil fades away. Like that voice that told me, I now want to tell you. If ever you feel spiritually threatened and all your other defenses don't seem to be working try saying aloud "light of God" and you too just may receive the protection you are seeking.

We Are Real

I had begun to question the existence of ghosts as my ghost investigating years pressed on. Since 2009, I searched for more logical answers to claims of ghost hauntings. My attention to detail comes from being a lifelong artist. I began to notice how wisps of breath or dust can make strange light anomalies in front of a camera. I, also, picked up on how subtle noises, that all houses can make, can be confused with actual ghostly noises. The more I began to think logically the more ghosts began to vanish. With every investigation I wished for something convincing to happen. Rarely does anything happen that cannot be explained through reenacting or review. I still enjoyed exploring for spirits, but there are two types of people that look for ghosts: those who believe in ghosts and those who do not. My discouragements began to add up and the rational debate I had with myself began to make my belief in ghosts more skeptical than ever. That was until an ordinary fall night in 2010 when I went to bed a skeptic and woke up a believer.

I was asleep and well into a dream in which a bright white fog that I was staring into surrounded me. I waved my hands about in an attempt to clear away the fog. I took only a few steps when the white fog began to dissipate. Shapes were appearing in front of me, and the further I walked, the more discernable the shapes became. There were people all standing and facing me. Maybe it was the remaining fog or just an inability within my dream see them, but all these people's faces were blurred and I could not focus on any of them. All my attention was drawn straight ahead at the center of all these people. I kept walking forward and when I was several feet away I could see a few in front of me step aside to let someone through.

Instantly, I felt the warmth of love for someone I deeply cared about. An older lady in a grey dress with pink trim had stepped towards me with embracing arms and a smile that was all too familiar to me. I felt so much love and comfort swirl all around me as I hugged my Grandma Del. Seeing my grandma smiling and laughing as we hugged filled me with so much joy. I don't remember exchanging any words with her, but I remember her repeating three words to me, "We are real!"

Suddenly, I awoke. It was as if I blinked and when I opened my eyes, again, I was in bed with the morning sunlight glowing from behind the window shades. The delight and excitement must have awoken me. I could still feel that same loving and caring warmth that I had felt in my dream. It made me well up a bit, but they were happy tears coming from my eyes. I replayed the dream in my head and could not help but wonder, was her message in some way related to my personal debate on the possibility of ghosts being real? It was not the most vivid dream or a very long dream, but the vision of my smiling grandma and her message to me has forever swayed my opinion toward the existence of ghosts.

I do believe in heaven and that my grandma is there. I, also, believe the souls in heaven can come back to visit and guide us all the time. Having faith in this I feel that ghosts and our destined souls are one and the same and cannot be believed in without believing in the other. The afterlife can be overbearingly terrifying when delving too deeply in thought on the matter. However, I am comforted by the fact that many cultures around the world believe in a heaven with a comfortable afterlife.

Not a Child

Some nights I have nightmares just like the average person. Most of the time, I feel they are brought on by my interest in investigating for ghosts. However, this dream wasn't induced from watching ghost TV shows or reviewing footage from an investigation. I have heard many stories of people bringing something home with them after investigating. Looking back on this dream makes me wonder if this was one of those stories.

The night was normal and I slept like I usually do; deep under the covers and hard to wake. I don't remember having any other dreams that night except for this one.

It felt like I was investigating for ghosts in my dream. I was in a hallway of an ordinary home. The sun was up because I could see the sunlight glowing through the rooms on each side of the hall and the sun was shining directly through a window in a room at the end of the hall. There was wood paneling on the hallway walls and a worn paisley patterned carpet, probably from the 60s or 70s, that lined the hall floor. I walked slowly and quietly down this hall, with my camcorder in hand, towards the room at the end. I could see that the room had a nice golden glow from the sun beaming through thin off-white curtains and the edge of a bed jutting out to the middle of the room.

Then I stopped because I saw something on the floor coming out from between the bed and the closest wall of the room.

It was a small child crawling on its elbows and knees. The child's thick, jet black hair was topped with a ribbon which led me to believe it was a girl. She wore a tiny t-shirt and a diaper as she scooted along the side of the bed with a look of worry on her face. She only looked at the adjacent wall as she continued to crawl.

When the child made it to where the end of the bed she stopped and slowly turned her head toward the hallway where I was standing. That is when she saw me. The child immediately had gone pale and her eyes went black. Her mouth had opened wide and her face stretched out as if to shout at me but made no noise. Then she became larger, looking like a gaunt, young woman. This sickly woman lunged at me angrily. I knew then that this was not a child, it was something else, quickly changing into something terrifying. In what seemed like an instant her face morphed from a child's uncomfortable expression to something so frightening that it startled me out of my sleep.

The story doesn't end there.

It was nearly dawn when I suddenly awoke, but my room was still dark. I squinted my eyes toward the window left of my bed where the morning sun was up just enough to give the outside light a soft blue glow. I peeked around the room. Everything looked normal but I had the strangest feeling that I wasn't alone. It was like that feeling you get from being watched with unseen eyes. Maybe it was residual imagery from the nightmare, but it felt like someone was standing right next to my bed.

Monument, Kansas

While gazing out over the overcast plains of western Kansas, I was passing the time listening to an audiobook as my family and I were coming home from a trip to Colorado. Western Kansas can have a mesmerizing effect when you peer out a car window and onto its flat landscape. Sometimes my mind will give me the sensation of flying over the seemingly endless horizon of fields and prairie. Only when a building or another car suddenly appears does my concentration break and I'm snapped back to the vehicle in which I am riding.

Up the highway, a lone sign appeared that read "Monument, Kansas." In the distance this small town started to emerge from behind the eastern horizon. My brother, Alec, and I perked up to watch the town go by.

Monument is a very small town. If you looked away for even a second you would miss most of it while driving by. What most caught our attention was a large building peaking over the horizon just as we passed the town's sign. It was a large, dark brick building that stood out amongst the small farm houses and old store fronts that lined its few streets. Looking past the smaller buildings and through the trees, we noticed that it looked like a two-story schoolhouse, much like the Farrar schoolhouse in Maxwell, Iowa, that we had visited quite often through our ghost investigating expeditions.

In an instant, the town was behind us. It went by so quickly that I didn't get a chance to snap a picture of it. Alec and I would have liked to have stopped for a bit to take a look but neither of us had been driving. We were left to only wonder until it drifted away from us. Alec and I always give each other a certain look when we feel a place could be haunted.

My brother and I have a strange awareness of nearby ghosts. It is becoming a skill that we cannot turn off. In a strange way we can sense them but not like a psychic or empath can. It is like a bell that rings in our heads, and signals if we are approaching a haunting situation. However, we could not tell you who is doing the haunting, what they look like, or if they are speaking to us. Maybe in time we will be able to pick up more through our senses. Until then, we just continue to perk up when we roll through towns like Monument, Kansas.

After a long day of traveling from Ouray, Colorado, we stopped for the night in Oakley, Kansas. That night I dreamed of Farrar and exploring its halls for ghosts. However, Farrar was different in my dream. We were staying in a white guest house next door to the schoolhouse. It was a small ranch style house. The house was run down and old inside. It looked like it had been there as long as the school had been there. When Alec and I went in to drop off our luggage and gear, I remember seeing clutter piled randomly throughout the house. Paint peeled off the walls and dust layered everything. As the dream progressed, I remember my brother's luggage and gear was in the middle of the living room floor of this house. It was raining and water was coming in and getting Alec's stuff wet. I went outside to find my brother to tell him that his stuff was getting wet, but when I came back inside the guest house everything was cleaned up! The walls were new, the floors were clean, the clutter was gone, and my brother's stuff was stacked neatly against a wall.

I was going to rush back outside to tell him, but as I approached the front door, a woman with her back turned to me appeared between the door and me. Her hair was long and black. Her skin was ghostly white and her dress was made of a thin light blue fabric that glowed.

The woman then turned around and her eyes met mine. She had large pale blue eyes that sparkled like jewels. Her abrupt appearance and stunning looks stopped me in mid stride. She was translucent and no feet were seen below her. Even in my dream, I knew she was a ghost. Before I could stare at her any longer or attempt to run away, her face suddenly grew hideous! Her eyes sunk away to deep black eyeless sockets. In an instant, her face and body became frighteningly distorted as she lunged at me. However, before she could reach me, I woke up and was back in my hotel room.

My brother was just waking and out of his bed, so I told him about the terrifying dream I'd just had. Alec recalled there being a house near the Farrar schoolhouse, but it was not in suitable condition to be a guest house. Also, it was located in the corner of the property and was far more than a few feet away. He immediately gave me a bewildered look and reminded me of the large brick building we passed in Monument.

A few days later when the trip was over and I was back home, I sat down with my laptop and looked up maps of Monument, Kansas. I found a street view map of the building that Alec and I had seen from the highway. Amazingly, the building appeared to be a school complete with a playground and an old house painted white, just off to the right side of the school and only a few feet away. It was the house I had seen in my dream.

ENCOUNTERS WITH GHOSTS

The following are a few of my most terrifying personal experiences with ghosts.

Rushville Schoolhouse

Rushville, Missouri, was the town where we had our team's first investigation. It had just been a few months beforehand when Alec, Gideon, and I were talking about looking for ghosts on a more professional level. Word soon got out about our new interest, and it was not long before we locked in our first location that was said to have some haunting occurrences.

A couple owned some land in Rushville, Missouri, that had an old one room schoolhouse on the property. When the couple moved onto the property, they found the schoolhouse was a perfect place for storing their things. It was not long before they began experiencing eerie occurrences when working around the old building.

The owners began seeing strange shadows and figures in and around the schoolhouse. There were a few instances when the owners reported being touched by someone when they were completely by themselves. One of the scariest events the owners had experienced was when they occasionally saw what appeared to be a man peering out the window of the schoolhouse. He would glance at them before disappearing around the corner or into thin air. The owners would often run into the schoolhouse almost hoping to find a stranger wandering around their property, but no one was ever there.

At first the owners thought they were just seeing things but the sightings became so frequent they began wondering if their schoolhouse was haunted.

The owners started to ask around to their neighbors if they knew anything about the property. They also researched the land to see if any serious incidents had occurred on it. What they found out led them to contacting my team and me.

We arrived with all the gear we had at the time completely ready and excited to investigate our first case of a possible haunting. We met the owners who were eager to tell us what they had found about the property.

The story goes that the original landowner ran into some trouble with a group of thieves that tried to take his horses and money. He didn't want to give up his horses or money and eventually the thieves lost their patience with the owner protecting his property. They took him to an old oak tree on the south side of the schoolhouse where they hung him to death. It is said that the thieves buried him eight feet under the same oak tree where he was murdered.

After hearing about the land's background and getting a tour of the property we were ready to begin our investigation. Our first location on this property turned out to be an eye-opening experience. We were out in a rural part of Missouri, and Rushville just happened to be right across the Missouri River from

Atchison, Kansas. Atchison is a town known to be Kansas' most haunted town. Our location was indeed eerie, but what we encountered throughout the night was even scarier.

We experienced our meters unexplainably going off throughout the night. We even saw some of the strange shadows peaking around corners that the owners were said to have observed. We had a stationary camcorder unexplainably turn on. A camcorder turning off can have some easier explanations but when a camera turns *on* even when the switch was turn to "off" left us completely baffled. We all had our own creepy personal experiences that night, but my experience changed my whole perspective on investigating ghosts. I was prepared for possibly seeing and hearing strange things, but I was not ready for what happened to me on the south side of the old schoolhouse.

While walking westward past the schoolhouse and towards a hill sloping downwards, I took a few steps down the hill when I suddenly stopped. I became motionless because I felt someone's hand grasp my upper shoulder. It was a rather warm November night but the sensation of someone clutching my shoulder sent chills through me, and I froze where I stood. I looked around me, but no one was there!

The closest person was Gideon who was on the west side of the school house, about twenty feet away, taking pictures with his digital camera. What Gideon said next chilled me to the bone. Gideon noticed me getting ready to walk down the hill and began taking pictures in my direction. At the same time that I had suddenly stopped, Gideon snapped a photo and looked at the picture closer on his camera display screen. That is when he called out to me, "Whoa, Adam! I think something is right by you!"

I stood in disbelief, first at the feeling of being grabbed, then at the sight of what Gideon had shown me on his camera. Gideon had taken a photo coincidentally right as I experienced getting grabbed on my shoulder. What appeared on his camera display was a large glowing orb right behind me.

Photo taken by Gideon Coyle

I believe that orbs are more often dust particles reflecting the camera's flash back into the camera's lens but this orb certainly made me think differently before ruling out all orbs.

Was this the form of a spirit captured at the same time I was grasped on my shoulder by an unseen force, or was this a piece of dust floating by at the same time I was experiencing this unexplainable event? I am not sure. However, what I do know is that someone stopped me from walking down that hill. I often wonder about that first experience and the sensation of being grabbed by something invisible to my eyes. Was it the ghost of the original owner keeping me from wandering on his old property or maybe another spirit guiding me to where I needed to be? Also, could that have been an entity behind me in the photo Gideon had captured?

Have a look at the photo for yourself.

The Knocks

My girlfriend, at the time, had just recently moved into a home in downtown Kansas City, Kansas. It was just a few blocks east of where I grew up on 40th street. The house was a typical home built in the 1930s or 40s, and was packed into an ordinary neighborhood with neighbors in easy talking distance in every direction. There wasn't anything special about the house other than the fine wood trimming and floors around the home that you don't see in the normal homes built today. Her uncle owned the house, but he was letting her rent it. I visited and stayed with her often because the neighborhood was in an area known to have a higher crime rate. She worried a little bit, but most of the time remained confident and often made jokes about the neighborhood to help her shake the concerns. Plus, she was only going to be there temporarily until she settled into her new job and made enough to buy a place of her own.

On one of the nights I didn't stay with her at the house, she experienced quite a scare. She immediately called me and shakenly told me how she'd heard someone tapping on her window as she was getting ready for bed. I quickly got myself dressed and was ready for a brawl in case some creeper was outside her house. Luckily, I didn't live too far away and made it over there in good time. I stayed on the phone with her until I pulled into her driveway. I didn't have much of a plan other than to find and attack the perpetrator. At the time, I didn't own a gun so I frantically searched my car for a makeshift weapon, the best improvisation being a tire iron. I grabbed it and a flashlight and quietly closed up my car.

I dipped into the shadows and made my way around the back of the house where her bedroom was located. I snuck about and stepped on parts of the ground that didn't make a noise. My adrenaline rose as I was about to reached the final unchecked side of the house. This part of the home was over grown with plants and trees but it was the side of the house that she had heard the tapping. I peeked around the corner and clicked on my flashlight. I darted my light all around but there was no one to be found. The ground and plants appeared to be undisturbed. The window was about six feet up from the ground, and one of the windows had an air condition unit securely attached.

I went inside and to her bedroom where the tapping was heard. When she was calm, I asked her to tell me exactly what she had heard and where she had heard it. She walked over to the window where she had heard the noise and mocked the "tap, tap, tap" sound. My girlfriend was a little upset, but she settled down after I checked all around the house, both inside and out. I stayed with her that night, but sleep did not come easy. I anticipated more strange noises like hearing someone walking outside or cars pulling up to the house, but I heard nothing alarming. The house made creaking and other settling noises, but that was quite normal for homes of its age.

Morning came and all was well. For a few days, everything went along normally until she heard the taps again. This time it didn't alarm her as much. She was already in bed with the lights out, the house was quiet. She listened for it again but nothing happened. She also listened for any footsteps that could be heard outside, but there was nothing but quiet nighttime noises. When she called to tell me about it she was handling herself quite well and said I didn't need to come over. I asked her to describe what she had heard this time. She told me it was the same "tap, tap, tap," but this time it didn't sound like it came from the window. Instead, it came from somewhere inside her bedroom. When she told me this, my ghost hunting senses were tingling. She knew I investigated for ghosts, but I wasn't going to joke about her house possibly being haunted. I suggested it was the air conditioner causing the windows or walls to creak when it cools. That very well could have been the case. Nevertheless, I became more attentive to the noises when I experienced them.

Her experiences with the tapping and knocks lessened the more I stayed. It also helped that she closed the door to her bedroom so that the window unit wouldn't have to work as hard to cool the room from the summer heat. My girlfriend would fall asleep rather quickly, I would stay up a little longer as I was now becoming more attentive to the settling creaks and noises of the house. The knocks, tapping, and other mysterious noises only happened every so often when I stayed with her. A few times I awoke in the middle of the night to what sounded like loud knocking on wood coming from somewhere within the house. I tried not stir in order to listen intently to see if

I could guess from where these noises came. When no more noises occurred, I would gradually fall back asleep.

Another morning at her home truly sent shivers all through me. I woke up, not because I heard strange noises, but because the morning sun was coming through a window and directly into my eyes. I flipped over onto my back and continued to lie there while my girlfriend slept soundly. I nearly fell back asleep until I heard "knock, knock, knock" clearly reverberate on the other side of the bedroom. I remained as still as a rock while I laid on my back. I peeked just enough to see the bedroom door opened, slowly moving to a gentle stop, as if it had just been opened.

A Hand

The night had turned into the early morning hours. Alec, Gideon, and I had just finished a Halloween event where we helped out with a public paranormal investigation at the Farrar Schoolhouse in Maxwell, Iowa. Halloween was still a week away but the schoolhouse was as active as it had ever been. While guiding people around the old building we encountered many strange things. Weird voices came through our audio devices and our meters lit up wildly in places where they shouldn't. Some of the event's guests even talked about seeing eerie shadows move across walls in rooms where people sat still! Farrar had always been an odd place for ghost stories, but we believed them. We had investigated it several times before and captured evidence that supported those stories of ghosts haunting at the old rural schoolhouse.

The event had ended sometime after 2:00 AM, but we hung out afterwards until about 4:00. We could not stay the night due to our plans for the next day, but luckily home was only three hours away and we had made the trip many times before. We were a little tired but we were quite used to staying up late to look for ghosts. I had driven us up to Iowa and had planned to drive us back.

Alec and I had started a tradition a few trips beforehand of grabbing some coffee before hitting the highway. The caffeine from the coffee gave us an extra advantage at keeping our eyes open during late night trips home. Gideon was included in getting drinks as well, but he tends to doze off shortly after packing up and departing from a location. However, I broke the tradition that night and decided to go with a pop. The night's exciting investigation had worn me out, and a fizzy fountain drink just sounded cool and energizing for the journey ahead.

The drink did its job for about an hour but weariness was slowly setting in. My body was crashing from exhaustion and probably coming down from the sugar high. It was a bizarre feeling as I struggled to stay alert both mentally and physically. I remember my body going numb as if it was already asleep, but my eyes and mind were still sharp and alert. I was expecting a second wind to kick in and that the sleepiness would pass.

Alec usually does a lot of the driving when we go out looking for ghosts. I had always admired his ability to drive home after investigating. No matter the distance, Alec's ability to stay vigilant on the road was just one of his respectable skills. Being his younger brother, I, too, felt like I had this ability.

However, this night was proving that I may not be gifted with the same ability as he, and it was just my pure can-do-attitude pressing me on. Perhaps it was my family trait of Tillery stubbornness.

My concentration was beginning to fade and my eyes were losing the battle. I tried music and snacks to wake me up but nothing was helping. I can hear you reading this, and my parents, too, saying that it is not smart to drive while tired. I agree.

The truck veered from time to time as it does for anyone who drives a bit fatigued. Thankfully, those grooves on the edges of highways that deeply vibrate your vehicle when rolling over them turned my focus back on the road. Well, I must have done it one time too many times because Gideon reached from the back seat and grabbed my arm as if getting my attention to ask me a question. His unexpected grasp jarred me awake and I felt my body surge out of the numbness as if being electrically shocked. I turned to ask him, "What's up Gid?"

As I looked in the backseat, I saw a hand, arm, and part of a vague face disappear between me and my view of Gideon... who was still leaning on a pillow against the window, fast asleep!

Gideon had not touched me. Nor did Alec, for I could easily see him in my peripheral with one hand in his lap and the other holding his coffee. I was now wide awake and freaked out! I gasped and gave a hysterical laugh as I swatted my right arm as if a spider were crawling on it. Chuckling himself, Alec looked at me startled and wondered why all of sudden I was awkwardly laughing. *I should point out that I tend to laugh out loud when frightened, strange quirk of mine.* I told him how I thought Gideon was looking at me and grabbing my right arm to get my attention. Alec turned behind him to see for himself that Gideon was still asleep.

We had conducted several explorations of haunted buildings and have heard cases of entities attaching themselves to recent visitors. Alec himself has a story or two of these attachments but those are better left for him to tell. It was indeed an exciting moment and the experience provided us with a much needed boost of energy to finish the trip home. We made it home safely and I half expected my highway fright to follow me into my dreams. I crawled into bed and slept quite soundly that night.

If this was a spiritual attachment from Farrar, I think it was just a ghost friend of Farrar who came along for the ride because it wanted to make sure its ghost hunting friends had a safe drive home. If that friend is somehow reading this now, I want to tell you we will be back to visit with you again and thank you for watching out for us.

My Name

It was a cool evening that night I brought my girlfriend to the Belvoir Winery. My ghost investigation team and I were volunteering at the winery's public paranormal investigation where we would guide guests of the winery around the property.

Formerly the Independent Order of Odd Fellows Home of Liberty, Missouri, the Belvoir Winery remains as the only functional building left on the property. Once abandoned, the winery building is now a wonder to look at. The outside of the building has been cleaned up and the owners have honored the building well with the restorations they have made. Visiting the winery and watching its many guests walk the halls will gives one a feel for what the place looked like in its active Odd Fellow days a hundred years ago. Besides offering fine wine, the Belvoir Winery also enjoys sharing the building's history with the public. The custodians have respectfully displayed the artifacts and documents pertaining to the Odd Fellows, the elderly, and the orphans who once called the property home.

The Belvoir Winery used to be an Administrative Building for the Odd Fellows who owned the property beginning in the late 1890s. In addition to the Administrative Building, there is a nursing home built in 1950s on the site where a school for orphans once stood until it was torn down. Also, to the north of the nursing home is the Old Folks Home built in the early 1900s which once accommodated over 300 elderly and orphans. On the northern most end of the property rests a hospital that was built in the 1920s. For a number of years it was the only hospital in the vicinity of Liberty, Missouri. However, the hospital quickly became obsolete when technology could not adapt to its older style of architecture, and the narrow hallways made it difficult to push and turn gurneys around corners and into the rooms.

There is also a cemetery, a ruined power plant, and other long forgotten structures scattered throughout the property that are gradually being consumed by time and nature.

I enjoy exploring those abandoned structures as much as I like walking around the winery building. The un-renovated buildings and splintered timbers of old worn down structures are like museum pieces to me that I can touch and walk through. I enjoy imagining what the empty rooms used to be and knowing that every sound these abandoned places make may be a potential ghost wishing to get my attention or possibly hiding from me. I find something new and fascinating every time I go up there.

That night in particular was a night the buildings just didn't intrigue me with their usual bumps, knocks, and creaks. That night they spoke to me.

Alec, Gideon, and I were leading a group of people through the hospital while other groups went to the Old Folks Home, the nursing home, and the third floor of the winery. My girlfriend was also accompanying me on this investigation and would typically stay near me because looking for ghosts was not really her thing. However, she was able to keep her composure while I worked.

A few of the guests needed to return to the winery and I volunteered to take them back. Alec, Gideon, and my girlfriend remained behind with the investigating group while I escorted the guests back to the winery. While there some of the other winery guests stopped to talk with me a bit about their experiences in the building.

Some time had passed before I headed back out to return to the group, but when I radioed to Alec to tell him I was on my way back to the hospital he didn't respond. I walked past the front of the nursing home and the Old Folks Home attempting to contact Alec and the rest of the group along the way but received no response. When I made it back to the hospital, I could not hear or see anyone in the building. I took a few steps in and shouted for someone to respond, but no one answered.

My radio chirped for a second with static. Sometimes it will do that when someone with another radio tries to communicate from a distance that is almost out of the receiving radio's range. I hastily interpreted the quick radio static as Alec and his rest group not being in the hospital. I left the building and began making my way back to the winery to regroup.

As I left the hospital, I noticed an eerie quiet surrounding me. There were plenty of groups that were walking around the property all night but no flickers of flashlights or chatty whispers echoing throughout the nearby buildings. The only lights were emanating from nearby neighborhoods. The large old hospital and even larger Old Folks Home loomed over me as I walked between them. I immediately felt all alone on the northern end of the property with the sensation of unseen eyes watching and wishing to draw nearer to me.

The uneasiness made my pace quicken. I tried calling Alec on the radio again but there was still no response from him. The Old Folks Home's unnerving front facade looked down at me with gnarled vines grasping at its dark red brick walls and rectangular pits of black where windows used to be. I'd walked the grounds many times before but, it is rare when I am by myself. One can really feel all the ghost stories of the winery suddenly close in on you.

I had nearly walked past the Old Folks Home when, to my relief, I heard my girlfriend call out my name from behind me. I turned around but she was not there. Next I heard the sound of footsteps crunching on tiles and glass coming from the Old Folks Home, so I wondered if she had called to me from inside. I tried my radio once more to see if Alec and the group was there, but he still didn't answer, so I walked closer to the building and shouted in a loud whisper up into the Old Folks Home. I didn't want to be too loud in case there was another group conducting an investigation nearby. After I shouted, I could still hear the footsteps shuffling around somewhere on the second floor. The Old Folks Home had been the next location we were supposed to be taking our group, so I assumed that they must have entered through the back door while I was out in front.

I backtracked around the perimeter of the Old Folks Home to its northern side where the entrance was. As I approached the door, I half expected my girlfriend to meet me there since she had called my name. There wasn't any concern in her voice or any discernable emotional tone. She said it as she normally would to get my attention, almost sing-songy. However, she wasn't there nor was anyone else. I was almost certain a group was investigating inside the Old Folks Home and was sure my girlfriend had called my name. If it was not her, then I was going to see who it had been.

That looming presence of many eyes watching me returned. I neared the threshold of the northern entrance to the Old Folks Home, but before I could cross it I was overcome with a sense that I should not go inside. I stopped and stared in to the blackness of the entrance waiting to hear footsteps coming down the stairs or see a light glowing off a wall, but there was nothing. Absolutely no sounds or lights came from the building. Now it was eerily quiet in the building and all around me. I clicked on my flashlight and shone it in the entrance, but all I saw were old appliances and dusty furniture reflecting back at me.

The feeling was strange. It felt as if I were on the edge of entering a nightmare with unseen hands pulling me in and distant voices pleading with me not to enter. Common sense finally took hold of me and I decided to just head back to the winery where I knew they would eventually turn up.

I cautiously walked past the Old Folks Home, watching every window with the feeling of something lurking in the shadows growing with every step I took back to the winery. I even passed the nursing home with a suspicious eye.

Rounding the front of the nursing home, the winery came into view, and the first person I saw was my girlfriend standing on the side balcony under a light.

"There you are! I've been wondering where you were. Where did you go?" she asked as she ran over to me with concern.

When she got back to the winery she could not find me anywhere inside so she had walked outside to the balcony where she waited for me to come back in. I told her how I went looking her and the rest of the group back at the hospital. She told me that everyone, including all the teams and groups, had come back some time ago and are waiting inside to go on the next round of investigating. I asked her if she was sure everyone was back and she assured me that they were all in the winery and had been there for quite a while taking a break. That is when I told her how I thought she had called my name near the Old Folks Home. Her jaw dropped and her eyes widened. A deep chill ran through me after what she told me next.

My girlfriend clung to me with a shiver and said, "I never left the group! When we left the hospital we walked behind the buildings. I wasn't isn't anywhere near the front of the Old Folks Home. When I couldn't find you inside the winery, I went out to the balcony. Just before I saw you coming around the front of the buildings, I thought I heard *you calling to me* from behind the nursing home!"

The Gas Chamber

When offered the chance to be the one of the first people to investigate Missouri State Penitentiary for ghosts, my team and I quickly accepted the offer. It was April 2011 when Alec, Gideon, and I made our way to Jefferson City, Missouri to meet up with another team that was also investigating the prison. This was going to be our biggest investigation so far and the idea of exploring a recently discontinued penitentiary thrilled us! We were used to exploring old American Civil War homes and abandoned schools. The locations within the walls of the penitentiary were places we would have to ask prison related questions and research what life was like behind the bars of MSP.

When we arrived at Missouri State Penitentiary they notified us that we would able to investigate A-Hall, the oldest existing building of MSP. This included four levels of tiny jail cells side by side stretching nearly as long as a football field. You could almost feel each prisoner's story as you walked by the cells. Most of them were open and you could walk in to view them. Some were plain with dull paints peeling off of the wall while others remained elaborately painted with scenes of life outside of captivity.

Underneath A-Hall is what was called the dungeon, the darkest part of the penitentiary. To access to the dungeon, one had to walk down a flight of stairs that led to a wide open shower room then enter through a heavy metal door off to the side. The metal door creaked open ominously and revealed only a pitch black void on the other side. When prisoners were thrown in the dungeon, there was no light. They sat in the darkness for who knows how long with only their thoughts to keep them company.

We caught many strange anomalies in A-Hall and in the dungeon. While exploring walkways and catwalks in A-Hall, we were able to capture a few baffling electronic voice phenomena on our audio recorders. Likewise, in the dungeon we were able to get intelligent responses on audio through unseen fingers tapping on the walls from empty rooms when we prompted the spirits to do so to let us know where they were.

The final location of our investigation was be the gas chamber. It was quite a distance away, but worth the walk. I could not wait to set up our equipment and see what we could find. Given that the place was made to put people to death, surely there had been some heavy emotions released there and still reverberating in the walls. I was so focused on capturing evidence of the hauntings that I completely disregarded the perils of the investigation.

There are many dangers you can run into when investigating haunted places. The primary risks are physical and you must always take your location into account. Looking for ghosts can take you to dirty, muddy, moldy, hot, and inhospitable cold places. It is always best to prepare clothes appropriate for the weather conditions and to pack extra clothes you don't mind getting soiled. Performing a preliminary tour of the location you are investigating will help you get a general idea of the terrain you'll be traversing. You never know how sound a structure is or how loose a board can be until you test it. Finding out the integrity of a building or the condition of an outdoor location while there is still daylight is best before exploring the unknown in the dark. People often ask why my team and I wear the tactical vest and combat boots, and we simply reply to them one of our mottos, "Geared for anywhere, ready for anything."

My team and I are prepared for any conditions we may encounter, but there are times we may not take into account the other less frequent dangers when searching for ghosts. I believe many ghost investigators truly enjoy the thrill of seeing or hearing a ghost, but we often forget about what ghosts can do to our psychological state of mind. If you follow and watch other group's investigations and evidence, or even the watch the TV ghost shows, they will sometimes talk about their minds and bodies being affected by what they believe to be an attack from some unseen entity. When this occurs, it is a very uneasy feeling and they cannot always explain why they feel this way. Other times it can be such an overwhelming sensation that it can cause someone to feel gravely ill or, God forbid, possessed.

I used to be completely skeptical of the idea that ghosts were able to physically or mentally harm me. However, that all changed that night my team and I investigated the gas chamber.

I ventured inside thinking how exciting it was going to be if we are able to capture evidence of something paranormal in such a location. While walking the stone pathway to the gas chamber we passed a large cross that was built into the sidewalk. It quickly humbled us as we approached the small building with a large slender smoke stack jutting up into the night sky.

As we stepped through the front door, we found ourselves in a small room with two jail cells off to the right of us and a giant cylindrical room, fastened together with hundreds of rivets, right in front of us. It was the gas chamber. Our flashlights darted about and captured the white chamber in an eerie glow as we filed in around it. Our eyes were drawn to the switches on the wall that engaged the gas into the chamber when it was still in operation. It was then we noticed a picture hanging on the other wall, depicting 40 images of the people that were sentenced to death in the gas chamber. Knowing that 40 people were purposely put to death just a few steps away definitely sent shivers through us.

While we considered the magnitude of death, our guide opened the gas chamber door. We were surprised to find not just one chair but two chairs in the gas chamber. The idea of two people being executed at the same time astounded us. The guide proceeded to tell us a story in which both chairs were used for an execution.

Two lovers, a man and a woman, kidnapped and murdered a child. Both were sentenced to death but not separately, so there were executed together. The woman was the only female to have ever been executed in the gas chamber at Missouri State Penitentiary.

After the guide finished telling a few more stories about the gas chamber, we were free to explore and investigate the building which pretty much consisted of two rooms: the gas chamber room and the viewing room behind it.

The viewing room was exactly that: a room to safely view inside the gas chamber while executions were being conducted. Family and close acquaintances of the victims could watch the accused slip away to death from bleacher seats encircling most of the gas chamber. The viewing room was small and nothing out of the ordinary occurred in there during our investigation, so we made our way back to the gas chamber. Other investigators were reporting strange vibes and chills in the gas chamber all night which made us eager to see what might come across to us. I may have been a little too eager. When the opportunity to enter the gas chamber became available I let my curiosity take control and I forgot to take into account those less frequent dangers. It was a mistake I'll never make twice.

I entered the gas chamber alongside one of the other team's members, but before I knew it I was taking a seat in the main gas chamber chair. The other member sat next to me in the second chair, and we both discussed what it was like to sit in a place where people had been executed. The other investigator eventually got up after sitting for a few moments, walked out of the chamber, and asked me if I wanted it shut. Thinking all would be well, if not better for my recording devices, I told him to go ahead and shut the door, but leave it slightly ajar. The idea of actually getting stuck in the old chamber scared me more than encountering a ghost in there. After he left an anxious feeling of wanting to leave began hitting me. It was a terrible place in which to be alone.

A-Hall was a sanctuary compared to the gas chamber building and I suddenly longed to return there. However, I ignored my feelings and tried to do some investigating while in the chamber. I recall saying aloud to myself, "What madness drove me here?"

I did not hear it at the time, but after reviewing my camera's audio someone had responded directly to my question, and the voice that was picked up said one word that convinced me that I was not only near a ghost but feeling them emotionally.

A soft whispery voice said, "Love."

It was distinctly a woman's voice, and the reason for her response was so appropriate. Only one woman was ever executed in there, and she was executed alongside her lover.

I began to feel a sense of dread overcoming me. I was starting to feel ill and didn't want to continue the investigation of the gas chamber. My teammates soon opened the door and saw that my complexion looked sickly. I rose from the gas chamber chair and walked out never to enter it again.

I consider this my most horrifying experience, not because I saw a ghost or heard one with my own ears, but because I learned the hard way that haunted places can affect you emotionally and mentally. Prior to the Missouri State Penitentiary investigation I scoffed at the idea of ghosts being able to get into my psyche. Now my whole ghost exploring perspective has changed. I felt it was a brush with death, but luckily not my own. Instead, I experienced what it must have been like during the last moments of the people who died in the gas chamber, and I have not been the same person since that evening. Now I am more sensitive, physically and emotionally, to the people close to me regardless if they are living or dead.

FROM MY HAUNTED MIND

This is a collection of ghost stories inspired by eerie locations I have been to and haunting visons of ghosts that manifest in my mind.

In The Corner

The sun streamed through the basement window. Caskets still lined the wall. The funeral home hadn't been in service for nearly 70 years. With the owner's recent passing a lone beneficiary was willed the home and all that was in it.

Harold had never known the 94 year old woman who owned the home, yet, somehow she knew him. It was just a few days ago when he received a call from the realtor handling the property. Harold recalled the surreal conversation with the realtor.

"I'm calling on behalf of a Ms. Florence Johnson, she recently passed away with no next of kin; however, she did have a will that included your name and address. She requested that her property be willed to you. We

also have a sealed envelope that has been addressed to you."

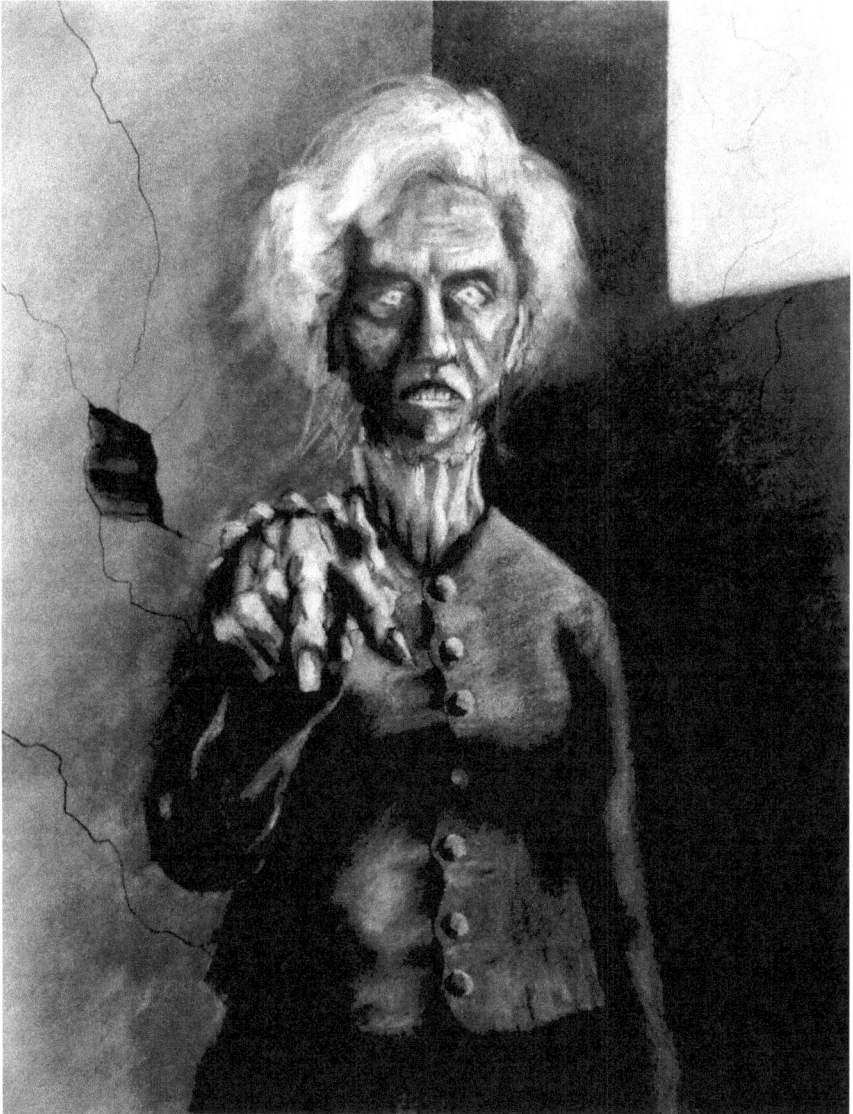

Harold was hesitant with the phone call at first. Recently, he had been the recipient of prank phone calls from his girlfriend who was calling him at night from an unlisted number. She would just breathe heavily in to the phone and never say anything. He called her to see if she was playing a joke on him, but the phone rang until her voicemail came on. He left his girlfriend a message accusing her of playing a joke on him about being a willed a house, but after meeting up with the realtor at the house in question he retracted his accusation. The realtor confirmed that an old woman had indeed left him the house.

Harold was handed the keys to house and a sealed letter left for him. When the realtor finally left, Harold toured the home and read the strangely written and very old letter in which the last few words had crumbled away.

Harold re-read the cryptic last sentence of the letter that accompanied the will as he walked down the basement stairs, "…and you will find what you are looking for in the corner of the basement where…" and then the letter faded in the deteriorated paper.

Harold sat on a dusty piano bench puzzled by what he had just read and the reason why he was willed the crumbling estate of an old woman he, and apparently anybody else, ever knew.

Harold chuckled aloud and looked around as if speaking to the old woman, and said, "In the corner of the basement where, where what?"

A crackly voice suddenly whispered from a corner of the basement, "Where you will find me!"

Harold's laughter abruptly stopped when he saw a skeletal old woman in an old dress pointing at him from a corner of the basement.

The Guest

Charlie had never seen a ghost but he'd always had a fascination for the supernatural. Any time he would find a place that had a haunting, he would want to go there and experience the ghostly occurrences for himself. Charlie visited many haunted locations and attended a few séances, but he never actually encountered any ghosts. He was jealous of people who said they did experience something paranormal and he became frustrated when nothing would happen around him or to him. Little did Charlie know that his wish to see a ghost would soon be granted.

Charlie and his friends were in a hotel lobby chatting about the séance they were going to attend later that night. A few of the guests at the hotel had reported seeing a spirit wander the halls. The apparition's frequent appearances were drawing in local reporters, and the reporter's newspaper articles were bringing in more curious guests like Charlie.

The hotel he had ventured to was far out in the country in an area known for its natural spring and mineral waters. Many people journeyed from all around to soak up the waters the hotel offered through their pools and baths, but Charlie was not there for the water. He wanted to see the ghosts people had frequently talked about in the newspapers, and he invited someone who might be able to conjure them up for him.

A few weeks ago prior, a man approached Charlie at a street corner in the city and asked him if he was interested in the supernatural.

Charlie was stunned at how casually the man had asked him. He was almost apprehensive in telling the man that, in fact, he actually was interested in the supernatural, but his curiosity got the better of him and Charlie answered the man's question with an affirmative. This strange man told Charlie that he conducted séances and would gladly offer his assistance if ever Charlie asked it of him.

The man's appearance startled Charlie. He was old and thin, and his face had many creases and wrinkles. Wisps of wiry white hair sprung out from an old hat atop his head. Tinted green glasses shaded his eyes but not the man's eerie smile. He held out one of his gloved hands and handed Charlie a tattered piece of paper with his contact information on it.

Charlie looked down at the piece of paper trying to decipher what it had read, "Ed A. Mand, Supernatural Séance Specialist," and an address unfamiliar to Charlie scrawled beneath that.

When Charlie looked up from the piece of paper to thank him for his offer, the strange man had vanished! He looked among the people walking on the sidewalks but he didn't see where he had gone.

When Charlie's next ghost excursion arose at this hotel, he immediately wrote a letter inviting Mr. Mand to join him and his friends at the hotel.

On the evening of the excursion, Charlie and his friends were having a few drinks in the hotel lobby while waiting to see if Mr. Mand would actually show. It was late afternoon when an odd horse-drawn carriage arrived and the wiry figure of Mr. Mand stepped off. Charlie looked upon him from a window while his friends snickered and snubbed at his odd figure and old fashioned sense of style.

Charlie greeted Mr. Mand at the door shaking his skinny gloved hand.

"Welcome, welcome! My friends, this is Mr. Ed A. Mand, my guest for the evening and this gentleman will be assisting us in tonight's activity," said Charlie to his friends.

One of Charlie's friends offered Mr. Mand a drink and another offered to take his coat and hat.

"No thank you. Kindly show me to where we will be conducting tonight's, uh, activity as you say. I need to prepare a table with some provisions I brought along. At sundown we shall begin," said Mr. Mand as he motioned to an old ratty bag he was holding at his side in his other gloved hand.

"Right this way Mr. Mand. I have made arrangements for our group to gather in a private room in the hotel's basement," said Charlie as he led the way downstairs.

A few hours later, the sun had just finished setting. Charlie and his friends entered the private basement room and approached the table at which Mr. Mand was sitting. It was dark with the exception a single lit candle illuminating a round table draped with a black table cloth.

"Please, gather around the table," said Mr. Mand, raising both of his hands and motioning for people to have a seat.

Charlie and his friends hesitantly made their way around the table as they watched Mr. Mand sit quietly staring into the candle. His green tinted glasses shimmered in the candle light and the wisps of his

white hair glinted orange like glowing ambers in a dying fire.

The room grew still after everyone adjusted as comfortably as they could in rickety wooden chairs. Then Mr. Mand began to speak.

"Let us begin," spoke Mr. Mand in a stern and melancholy voice. "Turn your attention to the flame before you. See how the feeble light flickers in the surrounding darkness? This represents your life. The more you stir the flame the more the light wanes toward the hounding shadows. Stir it too much and the light eventually succumbs to the darkness."

The candle light quivered as a chill came over the room. The shadows dancing on the walls seemed to dissipate as the lurching darkness swallowed them up. All was quiet until Mr. Mand spoke again in a more forceful tone, "SPIRITS! Heed the words that I am giving. Cross the realm of the living. Come forth from eternal gloom and join us here in this room. Bring your soul and ease your toll. Bring your soul and ease your toll!"

Everyone shuddered as the room stirred with drafts of cold air. Gasping whispers emanated from the blackest corners of the room where the candle light could not reach. Charlie and his friends became increasingly uncomfortable as the feeling of dread closed in upon them. He wanted to experience the haunting presence of a ghost but the sensation around him was nearly unbearable. Charlie looked at Mr. Mand who remained motionless and expressionless. He nearly told the elderly gentleman to end his séance, but then Mr. Mand turned and looked at Charlie and said, "They are here."

As he said this, he quietly reached over and grabbed Charlie's hand. Charlie wondered what in the world he was doing, then he saw that Mr. Mand was grabbing him with an ungloved hand. Charlie looked down to see that the old man's hand was a dead cold grey hand with thin leathery skin stretched over gnarled bones!

The sensation made Charlie jump out of his seat and he fell backwards, hitting his head on a pipe valve protruding out from the wall. His flailing limbs shook the table and knocked over the candle. The candle's flame licked the black table cloth and fire soon consumed the table! Charlie's friends ran to his aid while the others desperately tried to snuff out the fire. A friend called to Mr. Mand to help but he was nowhere to be seen. As the flames grew higher, things grew darker for Charlie. All faded to black and he remembered nothing until he awoke upstairs in the hotel lobby.

Charlie found himself standing there as hotel guests darted out of rooms clutching blankets and other personal items. They were running out the front doors of the hotel and he didn't understand why until he saw smoke and flames shooting up from the basement stairwell. The hotel was on fire!

He quickly scanned the lobby to find his friends. He finally spotted one of them kneeling on the ground, hunched over someone lying on the floor. The rest were there as well. Charlie ran to his friends to see who they were helping. He gently grabbed on of his friend's shoulders from behind to tell them he was here and that they needed to leave, but his friend just sobbed. None of them even acknowledged Charlie because they were so sorrowful as they wept over this person lying on the floor.

Charlie walked around them to see who they were crying over and asked, "Who is it? How can I help? We need to carry this…" and Charlie stopped short of what he was saying as he recognized the person lying on the floor.

"Oh, oh no. This can't be! THIS CAN'T BE!" shouted Charlie in disbelief as he saw his lifeless body lying on the floor.

Suddenly, the sound of someone laughing caught Charlie's attention amid the noise of people fleeing the hotel.

"Go look into the mirror, Charlie," said a familiar voice.

He tore himself away from the sight of his motionless body and sobbing friends.

"Who was that?," demanded Charlie as he scanned the room. I know your voice! Who is there?"

Then he recognized the lobby mirror and ran to it as the voice requested. Charlie gasped as he caught a glimpse of himself in the mirror. His appearance was frightening! His skin was deathly pale and blood streamed from his head and into his clothes. He followed the flow of blood to the back of his head where he felt the large gash under his hair and the dent in his skull.

The laughing echoed again as Charlie saw a figure appear behind him in the mirror. It was Mr. Mand with his head cocked back laughing and pointing at him. However, he was not wearing his green tinted glasses or gloves. Charlie noticed Mr. Mand's dead cold grey hand, the one that had grabbed him during the séance, revealing the old man's thin leathery skin stretched over gnarled bones. It was now pointing directly at him, but it Mr. Mand's eyes which terrified Charlie the most! Looking directing at him were two black eyeless sockets below which an eerie smile said, "Now, you have seen a ghost!"

The Watcher

My family had all seen the watcher in the basement out of the corner of their eyes, but no one ever had a good look at what it was. It always ducked back around the corner whenever we turned in its direction.

We felt like it was someone watching us, but always from a distance. It happened so frequently that over time no one really feared it anymore and was just accepted as a shadowy house guest that never got in the way. For me, fear turned into fascination. I wanted to see what it was that kept peeking around the corner at us.

One day, I pretended to fall asleep while watching TV. I would barely open my eyes and, occasionally, look at the doorway, but nothing ever appeared. The next night a big storm rolled through. High winds and lightning strikes were cascading all around. I was watching the news report on the storm when all of a sudden the TV blipped off and the power went out. The house was quiet with only the sound of thunder and howling winds creeping in.

Then I felt it, the eyes of the watcher observing me from around the corner! Being in the basement meant no windows for outside light to come in. It was completely dark, and the only source of light was a flashlight on a shelf through the doorway in which the watcher was known to stand. That uncomfortable fear I felt the first time I encountered the watcher returned.

I stood up from the couch and began to walk to the doorway. My arms extended out in front of me and my eyes panned the room desperately searching for a familiar piece of furniture to guide me to the flashlight I was fearfully approaching. Suddenly, I dropped to the floor writhing in pain. In my panic, my toe had stubbed the coffee table. I held my toe, gently rubbing the pain away when an electrical buzz went through the house and the lights flickered back on. Instinctively, my eyes darted right at the doorway I was about to go through in order to get the flashlight. A cold chill went through me as I stared up at the doorway. Looking back at me with beady eyes and a look of surprise was the haunting pale face of... the watcher! The thunder clapped and the lights went out again.

This story was actually inspired by a real experience in the house I grew up in. In the basement there was a doorway that bridged a library and a recreation room. I could face the TV in the recreation room and to the right of the doorway I could occasionally see what looked like someone peeking around the corner staring at me. I would get up and look to see if it had been brothers playing a trick on me. It never was them. No one was ever there. Also, this strange occurrence just didn't happen to me. My brothers and friends that came over to hang out also thought they were seeing someone peering at them from around the corner. We never could get a good look at what it was. I'm actually kind of thankful we didn't.

The Hanging Men

Roberta was so happy to have found an apartment for her and her son, Marcus. When she found out about the great deal on the living space she jumped at the opportunity right away.

Marcus was a good kid; he liked to play with his action figures and he loved playing basketball. He was excited to move into the new apartment since it was bigger than his old home, and he couldn't wait to build forts for his action figures and set up his small basketball goal on his closet door. His mom didn't mind basketball in the house as long as he played with a soft and squishy ball that wouldn't damage the apartment.

Moving day finally came. Roberta found some of her new neighbors really nice as some offered to help her move in; however, other neighbors acted strangely around her. They just looked at Roberta and Marcus through their curtains or simply stopped and stared at them with concerned looks upon their faces. Roberta shrugged it off thinking that they were just people who kept to themselves.

Upon the threshold of the apartment, she looked down at Marcus and said with a smile, "Welcome to our new home!"

Their new apartment door opened and a cold air conditioned breeze whooshed around them. Marcus ran inside immediately checking out all the rooms and admiring all the space. At the end of the day, all the moving was done and Roberta graciously thanked everyone who helped. She promised favors and treats in return for their gracious assistance. Roberta started by preparing a dinner for two good friends, Eddie and Sheela, who had helped them move in. Roberta thought it would be appropriate to break in the kitchen with her homemade meatloaf for which she was famously known.

Eddie went to clean up his hands and face in the bathroom before eating. With water in his eyes, he blindly reached for the towel, grasped it, and pulled the towel over to his dripping face that hovered over the sink. As he patted his face dry and rose up to check himself out in the mirror he suddenly jumped. Eddie thought he saw a man walking out the bathroom door behind him. He quickly turned around to see who it was but no one was there. The man didn't look like anyone he knew, so he brushed it off as possibly just an extra guest Roberta invited to dinner.

"Maybe he had just come into the bathroom and saw it was occupied," Eddie reasoned.

Eddie finished up and casually walked to the dining room table and asked, "Who's the extra dinner guest?"

Everyone just looked at him wondering what he was talking about, so he explained how he saw another man come into the bathroom. Roberta just laughed at him and said that it would be just the four of them tonight and that no one else was there. Sheela laughed at him and, jokingly, told him he was crazy and he was probably just exhausted from moving all day. Eddie reluctantly agreed with her and began to chuckle to himself. They all laughed while digging into

Roberta's meatloaf and enjoyed relaxing the rest of the night.

However, the calm night turned into a rather uneasy one for Roberta and Marcus. Roberta later came into Marcus' room where he was shooting a ball at the small basketball goal clipped to the top of his closet door.

"Alright Marcus, time to hop into bed. We're getting up early to bake cookies for everyone who helped us today," Roberta said as she tucked Marcus into bed.

"Can we bake some cookies for us too, Mommy?" Marcus asked as he clutched his Commando action figure.

"Of course we can, goodnight, my sweetie," his mother replied as she flicked off the lights and closed his bedroom door.

Roberta and Marcus drifted into sleep peacefully that night until Roberta was awakened by the sound of something hitting the wall in Marcus' room. She squinted at the clock that flashed a blurry early morning time.

"It is *way* too early for that boy to be up playing basketball," said Roberta irritatingly to herself.

The knocks and thuds continued until she stormed out of her room and over to Marcus' room. Roberta swung open his bedroom door expecting to catch Marcus shooting the ball at his basketball goal, but he wasn't. His bedroom light was off and she saw him with his covers pulled up to his eyes, which were wide open and staring at her.

"Marcus! Were you just playing basketball? I heard you shooting hoops and bouncing the ball off the wall!" Roberta exclaimed frustratingly.

Marcus just stared wide-eyed from his covers and said with a shake in his voice, "Th-there was a man floating around the room. H-his feet were sw-swinging and hitting the wa-walls!"

Roberta flinched and looked all around his room. She almost believed him until she saw the basketball lying on the other side of his bed. Roberta scolded him for lying and told him he wouldn't be getting any cookies the following day. Marcus tried to convince her of what he had seen, but Roberta was not buying it. She told him to go to sleep and she slammed his door shut.

The next morning, Marcus made his way to the kitchen, but he just stood in the doorway, not wanting to go too far in case his mom was still mad at him. To his relief Roberta had forgiven him and she explained to him that she had just been extremely tired in the middle of the night from moving the day before. She gave him a bowl of cereal and told him to go watch some cartoons on the TV.

Later that day, Roberta went out to everyone that had helped her move and dropped off some fresh baked cookies to them. While Marcus went to play at the nearby playground, Roberta went to the neighbors that didn't help just to introduce herself and to give them cookies as well.

There weren't any other kids at the playground when Marcus scampered in, but there was an old man picking up sticks and weeds around the bushes that surrounded part of the small park. He had pure white hair and wore a dusty black vest while he smoked from a long pipe.

"You there, young lad!" said the old man to Marcus.

Marcus stood at the top of a slide, looking at the old man and not saying anything.

"You're the new neighbor, eh laddie?" asked the old man.

Marcus just shook his head up and down.

"Howdy! I'm Tom, but you can call me Old Tommy. Everyone else does." He continued to pick up sticks and weeds from around the bushes.

"Are you the gardener?" asked Marcus.

"I am at times. I'm considered a jack of all trades around here. You know, laddie, you picked a heck of a place to live. How was your first night? Did you happen to see anything... strange?"

Marcus again shook his head up and down.

"You saw the spirits of this here land," said Old Tommy. "I reckon the tree which they come from was right about where you live now. Yes sir! A long, long time ago there was giant oak tree that stood there. Many bad men died there."

Marcus was entranced with his every word. Old Tommy spoke funny to Marcus and he wasn't quite sure what he was talking about. From a distance, Roberta called for Marcus to come over and meet a neighbor.

As Marcus began to walk away Old Tommy spoke to him again with a chuckle, "Hey there, laddie! If those spirits give ya any trouble you just give Old Tommy a holler and I'll come to swat them away for ya!"

Marcus made bounded over to his mother where she waited to introduce him to a neighbor. Marcus tugged on his mom's shirt and wanted to tell her what the gardener had said, but he couldn't get a word in before his mother started talking. Roberta introduced Marcus to the landlord, Mrs. Gray, who was so happy to have them as tenants. She told Roberta and Marcus about the how they were living in the most renovated apartment on the property. Also, Mrs. Gray told them that if they had any problems just call her and she would send someone over right away.

Marcus chimed in and said, "Mom, the gardener, also said if we have any trouble with the spirits that he would help."

Both Roberta and Mrs. Gray were stunned by Marcus' comment, but they just smiled awkwardly and wondered what he was talking about.

"The gardener told you this? Tisk tisk. That man," said Mrs. Gray as she motioned to one of her employees who was working on the garden to come over.

"Mr. Perez would you come over here, please?" requested Mrs. Gray, and the one called Perez hurried over to see what his boss needed.

"Mr. Perez, why did you tell this boy about spirits they *don't* have in their apartment?" asked Mrs. Gray sternly.

"No. I didn't say anything to him," said Mr. Perez in a thick Spanish accent.

"No, it wasn't him, it was the other gardener, Tom, over there," said Marcus pointing over to the playground.

Everyone looked, but there were just a few kids now playing around in the yard. Mr. Perez slowly backed out of the conversation and returned to work.

"Marcus, your imagination has been something else lately," Roberta said with a forced laugh. "Last night and now today you are talking about seeing people who aren't there. Silly child."

Mrs. Gray just smiled back and said, "Well, he wouldn't be the first to talk about spirits or ghosts. Ms. Estelle, your next door neighbor, once mentioned something about ghosts, but that is about the extent of the conversation regarding the supernatural around here."

Roberta looked over at her neighbor's apartment and saw the curtain slide shut just as she turned her head.

"Speaking of whom, I have yet to visit Ms. Estelle. I believe we'll head over there, now. It was a pleasure visiting with you, Mrs. Gray."

Roberta and Marcus departed from Mrs. Gray's doorstep and made their way over to Ms. Estelle's apartment.

Along the way, Marcus was given an earful by his mother about talking with strangers and saying foolish things about ghosts and spirits.

As Roberta approached Ms. Estelle's front door, it swung open even before she could knock.

"You are the new neighbors of apartment 444?" asked a fast-speaking woman adorned in charms and bracelets dangling from her wrists and neck.

She jingled and twinkled with even the slightest of movements. A colorful floral dress was draped from her shoulders to her toes, and upon her head she wore a silk head scarf that shimmered with gold and silver embroidery. However, she did not smile. She looked at Roberta and Marcus with either a scowl or a look of bewilderment.

Roberta began to introduce herself and Marcus, "Ms. Estelle? Hi I'm..."

As Roberta began to speak she was quickly interrupted, when the lady waved her hand in front of her in an enchanting motion stating, "I am Ms. Estelle. I'm a psychic and know exactly who you are. Your boy was not wrong last night. He had seen the hanging men."

Roberta looked at her like she was crazy. She was about to speak again, but Ms. Estelle stepped inside and slammed her door on Roberta and Marcus. Roberta was about to lose her cool until Ms. Estelle opened her door, again, and handed her a wooden stick with crosses, x's, and other strange symbols carved into it.

"Keep this near you at all times when you are in your apartment. It will help keep the hanging men away. Whatever you do, do not help them!" Then quickly and strangely, Ms. Estelle stepped back into her apartment, slamming her door shut once again.

Roberta stood there for few seconds longer in disbelief of Ms. Estelle's bizarre behavior until she took Marcus by the hand and walked back over to their apartment. As Roberta went inside, she promptly looked down at Marcus who was staring up at her with a concerned looked on his face. Roberta didn't say anything, she just stared back at him not knowing what to say. Then she looked at the stick Ms. Estelle handed her, turned it around, squinted at it, shook her head at it, then just walked it over to the dining room table and set it down. She looked up at the ceiling, as she contemplated about the things Marcus, Mrs. Gray, and Ms. Estelle had said.

"Foolishness," said Roberta, quietly to herself.

She then turned to Marcus, put her hand gently on his shoulder, and said, "Marcus, my sweetie, I'm sorry I got upset with you. It was our first night here and you were sleeping all by yourself in an unfamiliar room. I'll tell you what. After dinner we'll make some late night snacks. We'll stay up and watch a movie, and then you can sleep in my room with me. That way, if anything scares you in the middle of the night, I'll be right there to protect you."

Marcus hugged his mom and was overjoyed at the idea.

That night after snacks and a movie, Marcus had fallen asleep on the couch. Roberta picked him up off the couch and laid him in her bed, then went to his room to get his Commando action figure. Roberta stopped moving for a moment when she thought she heard something knock around his room. She listened for a bit longer, but no other sound was made. Roberta went back to her room and crawled into bed next to her son, tucking his action figure in his arms. Her concerns of the day drifted away, and she peacefully fell asleep.

All was quiet throughout the night until Roberta awoke to what sounded like someone talking in the room. It was Marcus standing on the bed reaching towards the ceiling. Just as she was about to ask what he was doing, her eyes adjusted to the darkness.

Roberta screamed and pulled Marcus down to the bed when she saw legs dangling from the ceiling and figures of men floating in the room! The men's necks were long and their hands hung either clasped behind their backs or limp at their sides.

Roberta then heard a voice call out. "HELP ME!" Then another voice demanded, "CUT ME DOWN!" Then another voice shouted, "CURSE YOU!"

Roberta grasped Marcus tightly and continued to shriek in terror until Marcus shouted out loud, "Old Tommy!"

Suddenly, Roberta's bedroom door flung open. A white mist filled the room and a voice echoed around them shouting, "BACK YA COWARDLY REBELS! BACK TO HELL WITH YA!"

Then all voices ceased and the room went quiet. The white mist dissipated and there were no more horrendous figures in the room or dangling legs from the ceiling.

Roberta frantically looked about the room while holding Marcus. She then looked at her son and asked what he had shouted out.

"The gardener told me to call his name if the spirits came back," said Marcus, shaking as he clutched his mom.

That is when Roberta remembered the stick given to her by Ms. Estelle. Roberta gathered her courage, picked up Marcus, and ran to the stick she had left on the dining room table. For the rest of the night, Roberta stayed awake on the couch holding the stick while Marcus slept next to her.

The sun finally rose and Roberta was still unsettled, but she felt a little more comfortable with the arrival of the morning. Roberta planned to pay Ms. Estelle another visit once Marcus awoke and ate his breakfast.

Roberta was cooking when Marcus finally woke and ran to her asking her about the night, but the protective mother just told him it was a just a bad dream. Marcus was smart enough to know that it wasn't a dream, but he could also see that his mom was still shaken from the experience. He didn't want to press her with questions about what happened.

Once breakfast was over, they cleaned up and went over to Ms. Estelle's apartment. Roberta prepared some cookies to bring as a "thank you" gift for the stick she had given her and hoped to talk with her a little longer about these spirits of which she spoke.

Roberta and Marcus, once again, approached Ms. Estelle's front and before they could knock, the door swung open.

"You saw them last night, didn't you? Quick, come inside; I have something to show you." Ms. Estelle grabbed Roberta and Marcus by their wrists and pulled them inside her apartment. Her tone sounded urgent.

"Please, have a seat," offered the woman as she motioned to a round table draped with an elaborate table cloth.

Her apartment was strange. It smelled of sweet smoke and spices, and there were old dolls and stuffed animals placed about, but they were not of the teddy bear kind. These were eerie things to look at and Marcus had no desire to play with them. Room dividers draped in all kinds of fabrics stood randomly around her living room. Candles, numerous exotic decorations, and old paintings were also scattered throughout the apartment.

Ms. Estelle disappeared behind one of the room dividers, then immediately reappeared with a book in her arms that she brought over to Roberta and Marcus.

She slapped it on the table, sat beside them, and opened the book, pulling out two photographs, and then reading a passage from the book, "The headquarters of the Red Legs was located in an area that became the old Welborn community, approximately, near 51st and Leavenworth Road, in what is now Kansas City, Kansas. The Red Legs conducted the hangings of bushwackers and other criminals just a few yards west of their headquarters."

Ms. Estelle looked at up from the book and stared at them both with a squinted eye asking, "Do you know where a few yards west of their headquarters is?"

Roberta and Marcus both shook their heads, "no."

"A few yards west of the Red Legs' old headquarters is, precisely, where your apartment is located," said Ms. Estelle, as she slid over to them the two old black and white photographs.

The top photo showed a large oak tree with many men hanging from it. Roberta gasped at the haunting image, then covered it with her hand.

"Don't show these to my boy," snapped Roberta. "He doesn't need to see things like this!"

Ms. Estelle was un-phased by her reaction and just stared back at her with twitching eyelids.

"This is ridiculous and you're just a crazy woman. This photo could be from anywhere!" shouted Roberta, as she pushed the photo away and continued to speak her mind to Ms. Estelle.

When she pushed away the hanging tree photo the second photo was revealed from underneath. Marcus' eyes were drawn to this second photo which was of an old man with white hair, wearing a black vest, and smoking a long pipe. The old man in the photo was standing next to a rope that was wrapped around a gnarled tree branch above him. Dangling from the same tree branch was a man being hung by the rope. Marcus tugged on his mom's blouse and pointed to the man with the pipe and the white hair standing by the rope and said, "Mom, that's the gardener, Old Tommy."

There are no records of ghosts haunting this area that I have researched, but the Hanging Tree was real. Before and during the American Civil War, there was an unofficial branch of the United States Army called the Red Legs. Their headquarters was near 51st and Leavenworth Road in Kansas City, Kansas. One of the major historical events carried out by the Red Legs was when General Order No. 11 was issued by Union General Thomas Ewing which forced evacuation of pro-confederate sympathizers in western Missouri. The Red Legs were a secretive group of union supporters who protected the Kansas borders from pro-confederate supporters who were referred to as "Bushwackers." When a Bushwacker was captured, and if it was decided that they be put to death, the Bushwacker was likely to be hanged at the hanging tree that was just a few yards west of the Red Legs' headquarters. My dad told me that when he was a kid, he had seen the rotting remainder of the hanging tree trunk before they tore the rest of it out and built an apartment complex where it once stood. That apartment complex is still there to this day.

Old Time Radio

The boys' parents, Chris and April, were bringing home the last of their grandparent's belongings. Their Grandma Emilia was going into a nursing home and their Grandpa Howard had passed away before the boys, Trevor and Toby, were born. There was too much maintenance for their Grandma to keep up with in her old house, so, sadly, their grandparent's home was going to be put up for sale.

Grandma was okay with this. The home she was moving to was closer to her children and grandchildren, and she was excited about making plans to visit them often. The boys loved their "Grandma Milia," as they often called her. When the boys started talking they didn't pronounce the E in her name, so Grandma Emilia always came out, as Grandma Milia. She loved the name. It reminded her of when her husband would call her "Em."

However, when Grandpa Howard died, the children and grandchildren were encourage to just call her "Grandma Milia" or "Grandma Emilia." She didn't mind being called "Grandma Em," but she became very emotional when someone, other than her late husband, called her that. She had loved her husband very much and missed him, dearly, every day since his passing.

The boys' parents, along with their Uncle Patrick's help, finished moving everything in the house. A few things were moved into the living room and dining room, but most of their grandparent's items were moved to the basement and attic. Trevor and Toby watched everything get hauled in, but it was the last item to be brought in the house that caught their attention the most. It was an old radio, like the one they had seen in the classic cartoons they sometimes watch on TV, and it was larger than any other radio they had ever seen. It was boxy on its sides, rounded on its top, with mesh speaker covers woven with golden threads that could still be seen glinting in the light. Jutting out from the front were giant knobs and switches used to control the large radio station scanner that was barely visible through its thick layer of dust.

The boys followed their dad and uncle up to the attic where they would be storing the radio for the time being. Trevor and Toby listened in as the adults spoke about the radio.

Chris and Patrick talked about how their mom told them to throw the radio away, that she didn't want anything to do with it because their dad died trying to repair the old radio. Chris wanted to fix it for his mom, but since it reminded her of his dad, he was going to keep it as a nice antique display piece.

The boy's dad toiled with the radio in the attic for a few weeks, trying to get it to work. He was able to power it up, but, unfortunately, static and various buzzes were the only sounds heard when he scanned back and forth for radio stations.

One day the boys' parents left to go to the store. Trevor had reached an age old enough where his parents trusted him to watch the house and his little brother while they were away. The boys used this time to explore parts of the house and get into things they were normally told not to touch. That day, they were eager to get a closer look at the old radio on which their dad had been working. The boys were told to stay out of the attic because many floorboards were missing, nails were poking out everywhere, and their parents always feared that they could fall through the floor or get zapped by an old wire. To the boys, the attic was a like a clubhouse filled with really cool junk that filled their imagination, and that radio was going to be their space radio to contact other worlds.

After the boys watched their parents drive away, they darted upstairs to the attic door. When Trevor opened it, the door creaked like a heavy wooden lid on a treasure chest. The boys climbed the unusually steep stairs to the top and saw the old radio in the back of the attic. Nearby was the only window in the dimly lit and dusty place. They dashed over and kneeled in front of it, staring at the shiny knobs and recently polished woodwork. They anxiously pondered a while on how to turn it on until Toby looked behind the radio and saw that it was unplugged. He found a nearby outlet and plugged it in. At first, nothing happen. Trevor was about to start turning the knobs when the sound of static, gradually, began to grow within the radio. Then, an orange light illuminated the radio scanner. The boys looked at one another and smiled.

Trevor and Toby began scanning the radio for imaginary signs of life from other worlds throughout space. The old radio screeched, whizzed, popped and scratched as they turned the knob back and forth through the stations. They pretended calling into the speaker as if it were a microphone broadcasting their voices out into the universe.

They playfully said, "This is earth calling space, earth calling space, is anyone out there?"

Still no broadcast was coming through, as they tried to receive a station with music or talking.

They played a while longer, periodically, checking out the attic window to see if their parents were pulling into the driveway. The boys had started losing interest in it when the radio seemed to be picking up something. They thought it was music. At first, Trevor was scanning quickly and musical notes were skipping in here and there. Then he turned the knob, gently, trying to dial in on the music they thought they'd heard. His gentle turns became slight touches as the musical notes became clearer. Now, they were hearing someone singing! Trevor gave it a few more light turns, when suddenly, music and singing blasted through!

"It's working!" they both exclaimed.

They listened to the crackly speaker to see if they could recognize the song, but they didn't. The music sounded old fashioned and silly to them. They giggled at the high pitched, nasally words a man was singing.

"If budding roses never bloom,
and gloomy skies forever loom,
I would joyfully let it rain,
If it means I see you again,
to spend all of eternity,
with my lovely, baby lady."

The music had ended and the static of scrambled airways took over. The boys thought it was so neat they got the radio to work. Trevor began tapping the knob hoping to pick up the station they found, but his efforts were in vain.

"I lost it!" said Trevor.

Right after he said that a growling voice, unexpectedly, came through the old radio with a warning: "GET OUT!"

The boys had just enough time to be startled and look wide-eyed at the radio when, suddenly, the thud of a car door closing outside was heard, then another door.

"Mom and Dad are home!" Toby whispered loudly as he peeked out the attic window.

The boys quickly covered the radio, scrambled down the stairs, and out of the attic.

They slid down the stairway railing to the first floor, then hopped on the couches, acting completely normal, as their parents came through the front door with handfuls of grocery bags.

Later that evening, when nearly everyone was asleep, the boys' father stirred at the sound of music being played. In bed, he turned over on his back and listened more intently, wondering from where it may have been coming. Chris sat up, thinking his boys were listening to music, but the sounds were not coming from their room. He walked to the hall to listen for its direction and squinted in disbelief when he realized the music was coming from the attic.

He opened the attic door, climbed the stairs, and saw the orange glow of his father's radio illuminating the darkness around it. He didn't know whether to be upset or confused at the fact that the radio was working. Chris cracked a smile as he examined it, but once he saw that it was plugged in he immediately deduced the boys must have been in the attic and played with the radio while he was away. There was no reason to wake the two of them now to scold them. Plus, if Trevor and Toby had not left it plugged in he may not have had the pleasure of hearing his dad's old radio working again. The music filtering through the airwaves sounded very old. He listened for just a short while longer until the music faded away into crackles and buzzes. He switched off the radio and unplugged it, pleased that is was working, but upset at the idea of his boys playing with it.

The next morning at breakfast, Chris confronted his boys about touching the old radio. The boys confessed after they saw that their dad was not all that upset. After a little scolding about being in the attic and playing with things they shouldn't, their dad told them that he was actually happy they played around with it because he was about to give up working on it.

Now that the old radio was working Chris was going to bring it downstairs to the living room, and the boys were delighted at the idea. Eventually, Trevor and Toby told their parents about what they had heard while playing with the antique in the attic, and their dad told them that he'd also heard similar old time music the previous night as well. He didn't, however, hear any strange voices coming out' of it. The dad chuckled as he found it appropriate that the voice told them to "get out" when they were not supposed to be in the attic in the first place. Chris ruffled their hair, playfully, and told them to finish up breakfast and get cleaned up. Their grandma was coming over later to visit.

Later that day, the doorbell rang and the boys peeked through the window to see their grandma smiling from ear to ear holding a container of her famous brownies which they enjoyed so much. April answered the door and escorted Grandma Emilia into the house. They talked about how nice it was to live closer to each other as they walked into the kitchen where April had a fresh pot of tea ready to go with the brownies.

Shortly after Grandma Emilia arrived, the boys' Uncle Patrick came over to help their dad move the old radio to the living room. After lugging it downstairs, Chris was eager to turn it on so his brother could hear it. He plugged it in, turned it on, and sat back waiting to hear the vintage sounds from the old speaker, but the radio would not turn on. Chris turned knobs and tweaked wires, but nothing worked. Frustrated, he slapped the side of the radio, then stood up to go find more tools to use on the radio. Patrick followed while the boys remained in the living room.

Just as their dad and uncle reached the basement, a whizzing noise of static gradually filtered out from the old radio. The boys turned around and saw the glowing orange light again, and the radio was working once more. It buzzed and whistled with atmospheric interference, but no music or voices came through.

Trevor and Toby boys were about to tell their dad and uncle that the radio was working, but as they were about to rush out of the living room, a voice crackled through the old radio and said, "HI BOYS!"

They froze in their tracks. Slowly, they turned around and stared at the radio as it began to play the same music they'd heard the day before. Chris and Patrick heard the music from the basement and ran upstairs just in time to catch the end of the song.

"If budding roses never bloom,
and gloomy skies forever loom,
I would joyfully let it rain,
If it means I see you again,
to spend all of eternity,
with my lovely, baby lady."

Chris turned to Patrick and told him that was also the song he'd heard while the boys confirmed it was the song that played for them as well. Suddenly, a crash of glass breaking in kitchen pierced the air. Before everyone could rush to see what happened, Grandma Emilia had burst into the living room as fast as she could with a look of great concern and disbelief on her face. She then astonished everyone when she began singing with the tune that was coming from the radio.

"I would joyfully let it rain,
If it means I see you again,
to spend all of eternity,
with my lovely, baby lady."

She stared, teary-eyed, at the radio while gently grabbing hold of her son's arm.

"That was your father's favorite song. He often sang it to me," said Grandma Emilia with a fond sadness gripping her.

Everyone listened as the music faded back into whistles and pops of static. The sounds of buzzing and whizzing wavered louder as if someone was controlling the volume. Chris, nearest to the radio, was about to walk over and turn it off until the loud static noise suddenly just stopped. The radio's orange light still glowed brightly, but no noise bellowed from its old crackly speaker.

Suddenly, a man's voice poured through the radio as clear as anyone's voice in the room.

"Hello, Em," Grandpa Howard said.

Clemons

Spring had finally made its way to the Iowa countryside. The land shimmered in bright greens and ambers. The foliage was just budding as the birds chirped and warm breezes whistled through the nearby pines. All was peaceful and picturesque, nevertheless, this calm landscape was occasionally marred with distant screams and mad laughter drifting on the wind and echoing through the valleys.

Standing out amongst the farm houses and fields on the top of a hill sat a large brick building that many of the town's folk referred to as "The Manor". The amount of people housed within the walls of The Manor outnumbered the whole town's population. It was the county's answer for the elderly and mentally ill who could not be cared for by their families. This also where the very less fortunate would be sent when none could or would care for them.

The building had existed since the turn of the Twentieth Century but the land was home to the poor, disabled, and untreatably insane for over a hundred years. Time seemed to be rapidly catching up with its outdated rooms and halls, and the staff found it difficult to properly treat the residents. The utilities and old equipment had a tendency to become faulty and occasionally things would strangely turn on and off by themselves. This always gave rise to the rumor of ghosts haunting the manor.

Stories of spirits had always been, teasingly, told among the staff, but the residents told ghost tales that were horrific. After listening to these stories, the staff would assure the residents that the spirits weren't there or tell them their own ghost story to make them feel like it wasn't just happening to them.

However, Rebecca Vored didn't believe in ghosts at all. Rebecca cared only for the residents and patients to which she tended.

To the manor inhabitants, Rebecca was their mother, sister, and friend. She worked as a nurse at The Manor, tending to almost every need of each resident. Rebecca often carried a bible with her and read to the devout Christians praying to be saved by God from their ailments. She and the rest of The Manor staff were considered saints by the townsfolk for taking on such a task.

The ailments of the patients varied, but most suffered from bouts of loneliness and catatonic states of living. Then there were some patients whose mental conditions left them quite unruly and foul. Those patients cursed and threatened the staff at all hours of the day and night.

One patient in particular, named Clemons, was so uncontrollable, profane, and terrifying that almost all the staff would refuse to work with him or they did all they could to avoid dealing with him. That is, however, all except Rebecca.

Clemons spoke very little and when he did it was usually gibberish. He was a mystery to the staff. Paperwork and records of him would occasionally disappear. No one was even sure how long Clemons had been at the manor. Gloria, the cook and the oldest employee, could not even remember Clemons since her first day on the job 30 years ago.

Clemons' hair was black and covered his face, his skin pale, and his eyes were dark like dry coals on the verge of igniting. Clemons was hostile toward the other patients and the staff. He frequently tried to fight his way free if he wasn't sedated or restrained enough, but strangely, he always contained himself when Rebecca visited him. The staff discovered Rebecca's ability to calm Clemons just a couple days into her job at The Manor, and let her manage him most. Rebecca often brought him dinner and talked with him even though he never replied back. Clemons would stand in the corner staring at Rebecca with a subdued expression while, occasionally, muttering to himself. At first, Rebecca thought he might have been trying to respond, but when she listened closely nothing made sense. She would just smile at him and tell him about things in the news and the events of her day.

Rebecca had a gift for communicating with people. All the patients wished to see her and be with her every day, and she was considered a walking cure to

The Manor residents. Her smile was contagious and her eyes were always gentle. She didn't even have to say a word to the patients to calm them down or help ease their pain. Her presence alone could bring comfort to patients and staff, alike.

One staff member found her presence more than just comforting. Dr. Rillard had been drawn to Rebecca since the first day she started working at The Manor. He frequently went out of his way to talk with her, pass her in the hallway, or conveniently placed himself near her any chance he could get. Rebecca was well aware of his advances, but she didn't mind. Dr. Rillard was handsome, charming, and always kind to her, which made her time at The Manor much more enjoyable.

All the patients and residents were able to enjoy a beautiful view of the large pond behind the manor. The pond rippled in the spring breeze between the rolling Iowa mounds and scattered evergreens.

On a routine day of transferring Clemons from his time out on the back balcony to his room, his behavior suddenly. He had broken free of the nurses and was making a mad dash through the halls and down the stairs to the first floor, all the while shoving patients and staff out of his way. He crashed through a pair of double doors and into the recreation room where an exit to the outside was located. Clemons almost exited through the back of the manor until he was suddenly stopped by Rebecca who had been coming back inside after taking a brief break. His sprint came to a sudden stop.

Clemons startled Rebecca, making her drop her Bible. He stared at the nurse while breathing heavily while his wide, dark eyes peered through his long disheveled black hair. Then he looked at the dropped Bible laying open on the floor.

In a rare occurrence, Clemons uttered something actually discernable to Rebecca. Looking up from the

Bible and at her, he said in a breathy voice, "Do not torture me."

He slowly bent down, picked up the Bible, and handed it to Rebecca. Other staff members burst through the double doors and tackled Clemons to the ground. Rebecca shouted not to hurt him, but they did not listen, and Clemons was dragged away, shouting wildly.

She glanced at the Bible that had suffered a few crinkled pages and smudges from being dropped. One smudge, however, wasn't coming off. As Rebecca tried wiping the page, a word caught her attention that made her gasp.

"Torture," she whispered to herself.

She continued reading on, "...and at the top of his voice shouted, what do you want with me, Jesus, son of the most high, God? In God's name do not torture me. Mark, Chapter 5, Verse 7".

"Rebecca?" said Dr. Rillard, startling Rebecca has she looked up from her Bible.

"Sorry, I didn't mean to make you jump. Are you okay? I just saw them taking away Clemons."

She smiled, shaking off the incident, "I'm fine, it's just that I have never seen Clemons act like that before. He actually spoke!"

"Here, come to my office and tell me what he said." Dr. Rillard put his hand to the middle of her back and guided her in the direction of his office.

Rebecca sat down and told him what had happened.

"Amazing," said Dr. Rillard as he stood up from his chair and placed Rebecca's Bible on his desk. His tall fit figure cast a shadow onto Rebecca as his broad shoulders blocked the sunlight coming through the window behind his desk.

"All the years I've known Clemons he has only mumbled. Now, he is quoting a Bible passage? Maybe your spreading of the word from the good book just might be having a breakthrough with our patients! Rebecca, you are truly a remarkable individual with a gift for engaging positively with these people."

Dr. Rillard stepped behind the chair Rebecca was sitting in. "Rebecca, I'd like to show you something and it needs to be a secret between just us. Step around my desk."

Rebecca had been entranced with the sunlight streaming through the window and onto his handsome facial features while he spoke to her. Her eyes seldom swayed from his or his lips which parted revealing his sparkling white teeth. When he stepped in closer to her and reached down toward the desk, she heard the sound of a drawer opening. Rebecca peered inside and recognized a revolver.

"If you ever run into any trouble here I want you to protect yourself. I don't want any of these patients to harm you. I really like you Rebecca, and I care about you," Dr. Rillard said as he brushed his hands down Rebecca's arms.

Rebecca looked up and into the eyes of his striking face and said, "Doctor, thank you for your concern for me, I do apprec-"

Before she could finish her sentence, Dr. Rillard leaned in and began kissing her. Rebecca was captivated, but pulled away and said, "But Dr. Rillard, you're married."

Later that day Rebecca visited Clemons while he was contained in the padded isolation room. She walked up to the door and stared through a tiny sliding window, observing Clemons standing still in a straitjacket in the back corner of the room. Rebecca motioned to the two male staff members standing nearby to open the door and let her talk with him. Clemons remained motionless in the corner but stared wide-eyed at Rebecca when she entered the room.

She spoke to him in a calm voice, "Clemons, it's okay; I won't hurt you. For the first time, I heard you speak and I could understand you, although, the words you spoke were things I wasn't doing to you. I have never tortured you, nor have I ever wanted to."

Clemons continued staring at her, with wide eyes, but he remained silent. She took a step closer and Clemons pressed himself further into the corner as if now fearful of Rebecca. She calmly raised her hand and gently brushed his hair off of his face, grazing his cheek which relaxed him. He leaned into Rebecca and began to weep. She embraced Clemons and comforted him while the two male staff members standing outside the door peeked in with disbelief. Nobody had ever seen Clemons express any emotions other than anger and lunacy.

As Rebecca held him, he whispered, "Go to the water."

She smiled after hearing him speak again. Rebecca asked, which water he would like to go to, but he just kept repeating, "Go to the water."

She assured him that they will go to water if he liked, but needed to know what water he was talking about. Clemons began pressing against her and was, gradually, getting louder as he repeated, "Go to the water."

Rebecca attempted to calm him down, but he still became louder. His face was now directly in front of hers, and he began pressing harder against her, pushing her against the wall with his lips grazing across her cheek. "Go to the water!"

Rebecca tried pushing him away to no avail, and the two male staff members rushed in to pull Clemons off of her. During the struggle Rebecca shoved his face away, but Clemons bit hard into the side of her hand. Blood profusely poured from Rebecca's wound and out of Clemons' mouth. The male staff members threw him against the wall and held him there, as he smiled sinisterly, while Rebecca shrieked with terror! His eyes appeared blacker than ever before as he glared at Rebecca who was clutching her hand in pain.

Clemons spoke again in a loud gravelly voice that didn't sound of his own. "You and the doctor, I know!"

Clemons' face was unforgiving, his mouth open with delight, exposing his bloody and jagged teeth. One of the male staff members struck Clemons over the head with a club rendering him unconscious.

Rebecca was rushed to the infirmary to have her wound tended. The shock and pain medication made her weary as she passed out and slept into the night in a vacant patient room.

Hours later she awoke when thunder clapped and shook the building. A storm had rolled in and was causing the power to flicker off and on. Rebecca stepped outside her room and saw two nurses frantically searching all the rooms that lined the hallway. She stopped one of them, Mrs. Tummins, and asked her for what it was they were looking.

"One of the patients has gone missing and we can't find him!" said Mrs. Tummins with a fearful tremble in her voice.

"Have the police been called and where are the rest of the staff members?" Rebecca asked, as she joined in the search.

"The phone lines are down and it's the night shift," said Mrs. Tummins with great concern. "There are only a handful of us at this time of night and we were unable to find the two male staff members! We assumed they were out looking for him since they were close to where the patient escaped."

Rebecca froze for a moment when hearing about the two male staff members.

Rebecca inquired, "Wait, two male staff members? Him? Mrs. Tummins, which patient is missing?"

Mrs. Tummins turned to Rebecca and hesitantly said, "Clemons."

Rebecca went cold with uneasiness and immediately ran down the stairs to the basement. Lights flickered at the crash of the lightning through the basement windows. Rebecca made her way to the padded room where Clemons was being held but found the door wide open and the cell completely empty. Blood was splattered on the floor and smeared down the door with a trail of it leading out of the padded room and down to the end of the hall.

Rebecca reluctantly followed the trail into the laundry room where it ended behind a large industrial washing machine. The lightning flashed again through the windows and Rebecca gasped when she caught a glimpse of a man leaning against the back of the washing machine. When the lightning flashed yet again and was relieved when she recognized the man as one of the male staff members.

He was looking behind washing machine when Rebecca called to him, "Hello! Are you alright?"

The man didn't respond. She walked closer to him, tapped him on the shoulder, and he still didn't respond. Rebecca grabbed his arm and began gently shaking him to get his attention. Then the man slumped over and his front pivoted towards her revealing the horror of a smashed in face! It was black and bloodied, his eyes swollen shut, his nose was pushed to the side, and his lips curled back revealing broken and missing front teeth.

Suddenly, an arm dropped from behind the washing machine. The lights dimly flickered and Rebecca's eyes focused, trying to peer behind the washing machine. She spotted the mangled and contorted body of the other male staff member stuffed between the washing machine and the wall.

Rebecca screamed in horror at the terrible sight. She quickly covered her mouth, but she was too late in trying to muffle her screams. From behind her echoed a sinister laugh. She turned to face the haunting image of Clemons wearing an unfastened straitjacket splattered with blood, staring and smiling at her with his jagged teeth.

His features had changed and were almost unrecognizable; his face had become ashen and gaunt. Through her tears of fright, Rebecca attempted to speak to Clemons, but before she could utter a word, he turned away from her and ran down the hallway. Rebecca shouted for him to come back, but Clemons disappeared amidst the flickering and flashing lights. Rebecca pursued him to the end of the hall, cautiously rounded the corner, and peeked into rooms, but he was nowhere to be found. Rebecca rushed up the stairwell to the first floor. As she reached the top, Mrs. Tummins grabbed her, frightening Rebecca even further.

"Ms. Vored, I heard a scream!" said Mrs. Tummins, flashlight in hand. "Are you alright?"

Tears streamed down Rebecca's face, as she told the older nurse about what had happened to the two male staff members.

Mrs. Tummins was shocked and comforted Rebecca, but told her that they need to get to an office and barricade themselves in until help arrived.

"Who is coming?" asked Rebecca as she crossed the hall and broke the frosted glass window of Dr. Rillards office. "We're miles from the nearest town. We need to stop him before he hurts anyone else. There is a gun in in the desk in Dr. Rillard's office."

She rushed to the desk and pulled out the gun from the drawer.

"How did you know he had that?" asked Mrs. Tummins.

Rebecca looked at her, but didn't say a word until she noticed her Bible still on Dr. Rillard's desk.

"My Bible!" exclaimed Rebecca and saw that it was opened to the page Clemons had smeared earlier.

Mrs. Tummins shone the flashlight on the Bible and looked at the passages to which it was opened. She leaned in and began softly reading the smeared passages. Rebecca stopped her and told her to again repeat verse thirteen.

"So he gave them leave. With that, the unclean spirits came out and went into the pigs, and the herd of about two thousand pigs charged down the cliff into the lake, and there they were drowned," read Mrs. Tummins.

"Into the lake, and there they were drowned," repeated Rebecca.

She looked up from the Bible and turned around to look out the window that overlooked the scenic pond behind the manor.

"Go to water," mumbled Rebecca.

"Mrs. Tummins, may I please see your flashlight?" asked Rebecca.

Mrs. Tummins handed her the flashlight, and Rebecca shone the light out the window towards the pond. She weaved the light from side to side until amidst the rain stood the dimly lit figure of Clemons staring up at them from a distance. Mrs. Tummins screamed when she caught sight of Clemons in his blood splattered straitjacket!

Rebecca told the nurse to run to the nearest house and get help.

"What are you going to do? You won't possibly kill him will you?" asked Mrs. Tummins worriedly.

"No, but I need to prevent him from getting away," said Rebecca. She tucked the gun into her waistband.

Before exiting the office, she went back and grabbed her Bible off of the desk. Mrs. Tummins found the other nurse and instructed her to stay with the residents and to make sure they didn't leave their rooms.

Rebecca ran out the back door of The Manor with the flashlight and Bible, in hand. The wind howled and the torrential rain poured violently. Rebecca shouted for Clemons but he did not make himself known. She darted past the back gate and down the hill to the pond where he was last seen. Rebecca panned the flashlight all around the hillside and pond, but he still he did not appear. She fought the weather to an old tree next to the edge of the pond. Rebecca continued shouting for Clemons and scanned the surroundings with the flashlight. Suddenly, he was right in front of her!

Clemons faced the pond as Rebecca shouted his name and tried to reason with him. His sinister laugh rang forth as she spoke to him then morphed into a maddening cackle the more she tried to communicate with him. Rebecca's attempt to console him was not working.

His recent actions and quoting of Bible passages led Rebecca to believe that Clemons' illness was not of this world. It was a growing fear inside of her that shook her religious beliefs.

She shouted, "Clemons! I know what is wrong with you!"

Almost instinctively, Rebecca began quoting the Bible, "Come out of the man, thou unclean spirit!"

Suddenly, the whirling wind seemed to hush, and slowly Clemons turned around. Rebecca expected to see madness in his face, but it was just the opposite. Clemons' eyes appeared normal, as he sobbed. Then he began to speak.

"I'm sorry," said Clemons clearly.

A sense of relief overcame Rebecca, and she calmly responded, "It's okay, Clemons! Come with me back to The Manor. I promise that no one is going to hurt you!"

Clemons continued to weep and stare at her with such sadness on his face.

"I'm sorry, but you have to go to the water," said Clemons.

Rebecca was confused as to what he meant by that. The rain whipped around them again, and the thunder bowled above them. Clemons looked up into the rain and began to speak words Rebecca didn't understand.

"What? Clemons, please, I don't understand!" shouted Rebecca.

Clemons turned and looked at her then, with something like a salute he tipped over and fell into the water.

"Clemons, no!" yelled Rebecca.

She frantically searched the water for him from the shore, but he never surfaced. The flashlight began to flicker and go dim.

Suddenly, Mrs. Tummins called for Rebecca from atop the hill, and with her were some of the nearby neighbors. Their flashlights beamed from the hillside, as they clamored their way down in the storm.

"Clemons, he jumped in the water!" shouted Rebecca up the hill towards Mrs. Tummins and the neighbors.

They were still too far up the hill to understand what she saying amidst the whirling storm. Rebecca knew there was no time to waste. She had to jump in the pond to save Clemons. Rebecca threw the gun and Bible to ground and dashed into the pond with only the flashlight still in her other hand.

In an instant she was submerged. Rebecca desperately waved her hands and flashlight around the water but felt nothing. The flashlight sporadically pulsed off and on, surely flooding with water. She surfaced to grab a quick breath and spotted the neighbors finally close enough to hear her.

"Clemons jumped in the water!" she repeated before diving back under the water.

Rebecca dove deeper into the pond hoping to feel or catch a glimpse of Clemons. She nearly surfaced, but with a last bit of life the flashlight turned on and grew bright. In the remaining glow of light, Rebecca saw the image of Clemons floating in front of her. She reached for him and noticed his face was changed and not his own. It was ghastly pale and his eyes were black with no gleam to them.

He sadistically smiled exposing his jagged teeth. Rebecca expelled all the air from her lungs, as she let out a gargled scream. Clemons grabbed her and all went dark for Rebecca.

The next morning the sky was clear and the warm spring winds blew through the windows of The Manor. The building bustled with the usual routines of staff members caring for patients and residents while the police casually wandered the halls questioning the staff about last night's events.

Outside, the press and locals gathered to converse about the horrific story that unfolded.

"I heard she was adulterous and had relations with some of the patients. They say she lured one of her patient lovers down to the pond to kill him, so he wouldn't talk," gossiped one local woman to a reporter.

Dr. Rillard stood at the top of the front steps and addressed the public.

"Last night, we had some ill-fated events occur at the manor. I'll spare you the horrific details, but what I can tell you is that a few of our staff members made a terrible mistake of releasing a very mentally disturbed patient sometime in the middle of the night. The patient was pursued by Mrs. Tummins and Ms. Vored, but, unfortunately, they were unable to detain this patient. The local authorities are currently searching the pond and the rest of the county for any sign of the patient. As of now, there is no sign of him. Nurse Tummins is currently at home recovering from the traumatic events and nurse Vored was pulled from the pond last night. At this time, she is still unconscious, but is being monitored around the clock. Thank you for your time and concern."

The doctor quickly returned inside the manor to avoid the barrage of questions following his address and made his way up to the room in which Rebecca was recovering.

"Rebecca? Rebecca?"

Rebecca heard her name called. Her eyes gradually opened as a voice continued to say her name. She eventually opened her eyes enough to see who was speaking to her.

"Ah, there you are, darling," said Dr. Rillard as he sat on the edge of her bed. "Easy now. You have been through a lot. I'm glad to see that you are coming around."

Rebecca groaned and tried to speak.

"Shhh... No need to speak. I'm going to take care of you, my dear. Here is a little something to help with any pain." The doctor slipped a syringe into her arm. "You died but came back to us. You coughed up a lot of water after your little late night swim."

"Clemons, is he...?" asked Rebecca with a weak whisper. She attempted to sit up but found her hands and feet strapped down.

"Hush now. The police are looking for him. Rest up because soon they will want to talk with you." Dr. Rillard gently stroked her hair and face. "Oh yes. You see, Mrs. Tummins told me how you found the bodies of the two male staff members by the washing machine and, of course, I know you went to speak with Clemons after you ruined our secret moment in my office. Well, I had to tell the authorities everything I know about the escaped patient, and that included your recent conspiring with Clemons. However, don't you worry your pretty little face, because when the doctor tells the police of your current mental state caused by your recent medication abuse, they won't take you away. They will keep you right here in my care."

Rebecca tried to shout and wriggle out of her restraints, but whatever Dr. Rillard had injected her with quickly began to subdue her.

"That's my pretty patient," said Dr. Rillard with an eerie smile. "Relax and I'll see you tonight after everyone leaves. Then, you can tell me all your troubles and I'll see what I can for you,"

Rebecca's eyes widened at the sight of Dr. Rillard's smile. His teeth were not the same teeth she had seen earlier. Instead, his mouth was blackened and his teeth were sharp.

"Oh, and maybe we can share some ghost stories later, too!" said Dr. Rillard as he exited the room, continuing to stare at her with his chilling smile.

As he closed the door behind him, a figure suddenly appeared in the corner of the room. The figure's face was long with the grave expression of dread; its eyes were sunken, its mouth hung low, and it wore a blood splattered straitjacket. Rebecca began fidgeting violently and screamed with only a weak gasp, "Clemons!"

Clawfoot Bathtub

Roger and his friend, Stan, strained themselves to haul a vintage clawfoot bathtub from an old abandoned hospital. There were "No Trespassing" signs posted everywhere on the property, but they didn't care. Roger wanted this tub. It would be the perfect addition to his new home and his wife would love it. They knew the property was rarely checked and the place was sure to be condemned, so Roger found no harm in salvaging an old tub.

Roger had discovered the tub a few weeks beforehand when he and his wife went on a public ghost hunt of the property. His wife, Patricia, really liked the tub and Roger toyed with the idea of sneaking onto the property and stealing it for her. She laughed at the idea and didn't think he was serious. Plus, she questioned having a bathtub from a haunted building in their house, especially after hearing stories told by the ghost hunting guide.

"Hey, what if the tub is haunted? What are you going to do then?" asked Stan jokingly as they slid the heavy tub in the back of Roger's truck.

Roger laughed through his grunts and pushes of the tub and responded to Stan, "Well, then you will be the first one I call to help me tote it back here."

They both laughed and quietly drove away from the old hospital.

On the way home, Roger recalled the stories told by the guide who talked about how the tub was in a bathroom used to clean patients who were incapable of bathing themselves.

"The patients were either very elderly, feeble from an illness, or mentally incapacitated to the point of being unable to care for themselves. However, the bathtub came with a chilling tale. It is said that three nurses drowned in the tub by causes unknown. They were all found with their heads submerged under the water, their eyes were closed, and there were no signs of a struggle. It was as if they were taking a bath themselves, had fallen asleep in the water, and drowned. The one suspicious fact was that the nurses had all died while bathing one certain patient. This patient was said to be an older woman with a severe mental disorder that kept her immobile and unwilling to speak. Early examinations of this patient revealed her body to be completely healthy but she was just reluctant to move, speak, or do anything on her own. The nurses kept a record of every patient's bath time. While bathing this particular patient, the records showed that every time a nurse had died the old woman would always be found back in her room, lying in her bed, with the lights off and the window curtains closed. How she had arrived back in her room was a mystery to the hospital staff. After the third nurse's death, this patient was handled by two or more nurses, at all times. Shortly after this, the patient's own mysterious death occurred in this very bathtub. None of the nurses could explain it. This patient appeared to have died like the other nurses who had drowned, only

the old woman's mouth stretched across her face with a contorted grin and wide open eyes staring upwards."

The ghost hunter's stories were truly disturbing, but Roger and Patricia were skeptical. They didn't believe the stories without seeing the historical facts for themselves to back it up. All they saw was a vintage clawfoot bathtub that would look great in their bathroom.

It was nearly 3:00 AM when Roger's wife awoke to the sound of her husband and Stan pulling the bathtub off the back of the truck. The tub's heavy iron and porcelain body clanged and dragged loudly as they struggled to haul it into the garage. Patricia was very upset with Roger, but he convinced her that the tub would be restored and would give her that designer vintage bathroom look, making her the envy of her friends.

A few weeks later the tub was restored and installed. Patricia's friends were indeed jealous and wanted to know where they had found such a tub, but she just told everyone that Roger had found it at a thrift store. Roger put the final touches to the plumbing and that night Patricia was eager to hop in and soak in the tub's elegant contours. In Patricia's excitement, she had nearly forgotten the tub's history and only saw the perfect addition of a rare clawfoot bathtub in her newly decorated vintage-style bathroom.

Patricia turned the hot water on all the way and let it fill up. The tub was steaming nicely when she removed her robe and stepped inside. The temperature was just right for her as she submerged her body into the hot water and laid back. At first, the water was relaxing as it continued to stream in, but when she turned off the water it quickly cooled. It cooled off so quickly, in fact, that it became rapidly cold and made

Patricia uncomfortable to the point she had to come out.

Disappointed, she drained the tub and filled it again with hot water. To Patricia's relief the water stayed warmer for much longer, and she found the tub so comfortable that she began nodding off. She was nearly asleep when she suddenly found herself unable to breath. She had dozed off and didn't realize that her mouth and nose had slipped under the water. Patricia tried to move but she could not and strangely the water suddenly became chilled again. That is when she felt something move under the water.

Something brushed down from Patricia's shoulders and past her legs. With her panicked eyes still above water, she looked at the other end of the tub when something began to poke out of the water near her feet. Patricia screamed with whatever air she had left in her lungs, and at last, she was able to move and breathe again. She splashed water everywhere as she flailed her arms and legs to clamber out of the tub.

Roger came rushing in see what the commotion was all about. He found Patricia gasping for air on the ground and crawling towards him. He threw a towel around her and comforted her while he asked what happened, but Patricia only wanted out of the bathroom. She bolted from Roger's arms, and he dashed after her to their bedroom.

"Sweetie what is the matter? What is wrong? Please, talk to me!" Roger begged as Patricia ran to the bed and hid under the covers.

Roger slid over to her and sat next to her on the bed. Patricia was shaking uncontrollably as she slid the bed cover down past her eyes. She looked over Roger's shoulder and down the hallway toward the bathroom. Then with tear-filled eyes she looked up at him and said, "Th-there was a wo-woman in the tub wi-with m-me!"

Roger flinched backwards and nearly smirked when she told him this.

"I want th-that tub out of this house!" demanded Patricia as she clutched onto Roger.

Roger told her to stay in the bed as he went to the bathroom to look at the tub. Nothing seemed out of the ordinary in the bathroom except for the water everywhere on the floor. He looked inside the tub, but only a thick layer of bubbles sat on top of the water that remained and Roger couldn't see anything beneath them. He waved his hands under the bubbles but he felt nothing but cold water. Roger went back to Patricia and told her nothing was in the tub, but she just continued to shiver under the bed sheets.

Roger returned to the bathroom to mop up the water. When he was finished cleaning up he walked back over to the tub and noticed the bubbles had dissipated. Just as he was about reach in and pull the plug to drain the tub he was startled by something he saw beneath the water. Roger leaned over the tub and peered through the water ripples to see an old woman with a contorted grin stretching across her face and wide open eyes staring up at him.

The next day, Roger and Stan hauled the old claw foot tub back to the old hospital.

The Ghost Bike

There was a church nestled in the inner-city among many urban neighborhoods, a prized location for the neighborhood children because of its large parking lot which was great for riding bikes, and there was also a playground with a large yard that the children used for playing baseball or football. The church was like any other modern one built in the 1970s. The sanctuary was on the top floor, a dining hall was beneath it on the level below that included a stage for performances, and there were two levels of rooms jutting out from the church's south side used for classrooms, daycare, offices, game rooms, and even a smaller chapel.

Over the years the congregation began to decline. Families moved further out of the city as land became developed, older members faded away, and the crime rate around the neighborhood was steadily increasing.

Sadly, these factors dwindled the number of attending parishioners. The church did limp on for a while by renting out the church sanctuary, the dining hall, and the classrooms out to local organizations. The church, also occasionally hosted neighborhood events that helped the church bring in a few new members and helped bolster the youth group.

Every year the church put on a Halloween party for the neighborhood, and the children loved it. There were games, food, and even a haunted house that led people from the stage at the end of the dining hall, up the side stairs, to the main entrance on the second floor. Long lines would form for this feature attraction. The youth group kids especially enjoyed the haunted house since they were the ones putting it on.

While setting everything up for the Halloween party, the kids would play around and try to scare one another by jumping out at each other or by making ghostly noises from hiding places. The season always excited them with the thrill of scaring or being scared. This was fun and easy for them to do when their friends or adults were nearby, but when they found themselves alone in certain parts of the church the building could become eerily quiet. The unsettling feeling of someone getting ready to jump out at you could be felt even when you knew no one else was around.

Stories of ghosts in the building had circulated ever since the church had been built. There had been old stories about a maintenance man who died in the basement rumors of people being found dead on the church property. One story the kids from both the neighborhood and the youth group kids could relate to was the one about a ghost bike that had been seen both outside and inside the church. Sometimes it would be seen in the parking lot after having been ridden by an unseen rider, or it would be lying down in the yard or propped up against a tree. More terrifying than that was the occasional haunting sound of an old bike bell ringing, "RING CHING, RING CHING."

The adults kindly played off the stories of ghosts in the church since they wanted to keep the building as invitin, as possible. However, some of them did wonder about the mysterious bike, and they had an idea as to who the owner had been. Some members said it was the bike of a neighborhood paper boy who had gone missing years ago. Other people said it was the ghost of a parishioner who had lived in the neighborhood and was hit by a car on her way to church just a few years after it was built.

After the Halloween party at the church, the youth group hosted a sleepover in the building that was filled with fun and rarely missed. Board games, pizza, and soft drinks were all things for the youth group to look forward to, but hide-and-go-seek was the most anticipated game of the night. The building with its many rooms made it an ideal location for the game. The chapel and offices were off-limits, so plotting the perfect hiding spot in the bevy of other rooms consumed the kids' minds all day and into the evening.

When the youth group finished cleaning up after the Halloween party, had dinner, and played a few board games, it finally became the perfect time to play hide-and-go-seek. Unfortunately, one of the kids had to be "it", the person whose job in the game was to go find and tag the others before they touched the "base" which had been designated as a table in the dining hall.

After several rounds of the game that unfortunate time to be "it" came to Ralph. While he hid his eyes and began counting the other kids scattered to their hiding places.

"Re-ready or not here I come" shouted Ralph as he scanned the dining hall for someone hiding.

His excitement soon faded as he looked out into a dark dining hall with the sound of his breathing all that was audible. He slowly stepped away from the base and quietly searched around the dining hall. He approached the stage with a sneaking suspicion as the stage curtains swayed a bit, leading him to believe someone was hiding behind them.

Ralph dashed to the stage and pulled open the curtain saying, "Gotcha!"

He jumped back and looked across the stage when he realized no one was there. Before fear overcame him, he heard a giggle come from the main hall.

"Ah ha, someone must be there," he said to himself quietly.

He dashed out of the dark dining hall and into the hallway near the lower level entrance where a safety light was always illuminated.

"I heard you and you're not going to get past me!" called Ralph in playful manner.

His voice echoed down the long hall but no one made a single noise. Ralph stood under the light and stared down the long hallway, anticipating someone to jump out at him. Suddenly, an unexpected noise on the other end of the hall broke the silence.

"Ring-ching"

Ralph peered down the dark hall, hesitating to chase after the sound.

"Nice try! You can't trick me into coming down there just so you could sneak past me," Ralph chuckled. But his laughter stopped when he heard the noise again.

"Ring-ching"

The ringing came closer, but Ralph still could not see anyone emerging from the dark hallway. Just as he was about to take a few steps down the hall, a figure materialized in the darkness and was coming at him very fast. Ralph stood ready to tag whomever it was until he saw what was coming at him from down the hallway. It was a boy on a bike wearing a red cape and a hood with devil horns on the top. The boy sped past Ralph, nearly hitting him. Ralph jumped out of the way and heard the rider giggle at him as he rode away and then turned into the dining hall. Ralph could not tell who it was. The rider had flown by so fast that his face was unrecognizable. Ralph shook off the sudden fright and chased after him.

"That's cheating!" shouted Ralph as he pursued the rider. "You can't use a bike indoors, and you can't use it to help you get to base!"

Looking around the dining hall once again, Ralph stood in disbelief. He looked towards the base then all around the hall, but he was completely alone. Just then, two other kids startled Ralph as they darted past him to reach the base. He didn't even try to tag them because he was so puzzled about who rode the bike past him and then disappeared. Ralph questioned the two kids about the rider, but they had no idea who Ralph was talking about. Soon the adults came out telling the kids to wrap up the game and that it was time to turn in for the night.

For the rest of the night Ralph wondered which one of his friends had been the bike rider. That night the adults and youth group slept in the parlor, a large room that was able to accommodate everyone. As they were settling in, tucking themselves into sleeping bags, and turning on flashlights, one of the kids suggested telling ghost stories. Normally, the older church members would be opposed to telling ghost stories in the church, but the younger adults who were supervising the sleepover were quite fine with the idea and even told a few tales themselves.

Silly ghost stories, spooky ghost stories, and even ghost stories that had been circulating around the church for years were told that night. However, one story in particular would change the rest of the evening and make it a very restless night for Ralph.

After hearing the story, Ralph shocked the adults when told them what he had seen while playing hide-and-go-seek earlier that evening. He shivered uncontrollably after recounting his experience, and the rest of the kids cringed at every strange noise echoing down the long dark hall just outside the parlor for the rest of the night.

The story was told by one of the older youth chaperones who had heard it years beforehand when he had been a youngster in the youth group:

"I'm sure you all know the stories of people seeing a ghost bike lying about or riding itself around the church. Well, this story was told to my youth group years ago in this very room. The maintenance man was working late and stopped in to tell the tale as we were settling in for the night. He'd overheard us talking about the ghost bike and he wanted to chime in with his own story about the bike, a story that made it seem like it all could have really happened. Here is what I remember from that night:"

They say the ghost bike belonged to a boy who died while trick-or-treating on Halloween. The boy was riding around the neighborhood, going door to door to get candy just like any other trick-or-treater, but he stopped just before he was about to ride past the church. The lower level entrance light always stayed on and the boy must have thought the church was handing out candy. Being a rather large church, he thought they would be handing out big bags of candy, of course. The boy rode his bike up to the lower level entrance and knocked on the two glass doors saying, "Trick-or-treat!"

To his surprise, the old maintenance man came to the door and let him in to get candy. However, the fact was that there was no one working or staying at the church that night. People claim the one who'd answered the door was the old maintenance man's ghost, and the boy never came out!

A week later, the church members found a bike tucked deep in the basement behind a large furnace. Since it matched the description of the bike the child that had gone missing had been riding, the authorities were called in. Police searched the building and questioned everyone, but the boy was never found and no one was ever charged. The only clues besides the bike were a few candy wrappers found just outside the furnace room door. The last known descriptive whereabouts for the boy had been, "Last seen trick-or-treating and riding his bike into the church parking lot wearing a red cape and a hood with devil horns on top."

The Halloween House

There was a time when the neighborhood thrived, when old couples and new parents with their children alike once filled every house on the block. Their yards were kept tidy and everyone decorated for the holidays.

Halloween was one of those holidays in which all the neighbors looked forward. The children would talk about Halloween all year long because of how wonderful it was in the neighborhood. Almost everyone handed out candy, and even if they didn't they would still hang up a few decorations during the season. Jack-o-lanterns, black cats, ghosts in trees and windows, and spooky lights could be seen all up and down the block.

It was like this for many years, but as neighbors became older and children grew the neighborhood began to decline. The older homes became harder to maintain and nearby crime began to creep in. Soon, the neighborhood's once charming appeal was lost as homes fell into disrepair, yards became unkempt, and the newer neighbors became unsure and sketchy toward one another. The holidays were never the same. On Halloween people became more shuttered in. The parade of trick-or-treaters gradually became just a trickle of kids barely dressed in costumes and with pillowcases for candy sacks.

Year after year and one by one, the porch lights remained off on Halloween, all except for one: Dolores. The oldest neighbor on the block still decorated for Halloween and handed out candy on the holiday. The children, and even a few adults of the neighborhood, affectionately called Dolores' house, "the Halloween House".

In the neighborhood's early years Dolores' home was always a main attraction on the block. She and her husband decorated the yard with creepy signs shaped like arrows with "CANDY" scribbled on them, pointing to the front porch. Wooden tombstones also dotted the front and side yards. Ghosts made of old bedsheets hung in the trees and several stuffed dummies made of waded up newspapers, worn out clothes, and old Halloween masks stood in the side yard. Dolores' husband would like to dress as one of the dummies and watch all the trick-or-treaters come through on Halloween, but you could never tell which one was him. As soon as the sun set, the old couple would flip on their porch light and wait for the trick-or-treaters to come rushing up their yard.

Those dummies were an odd but enjoyable attraction to trick-or-treaters, although not many dared to approach them because they looked real enough to reach out and grab you. To the trick-or-treaters they stood very still but seemed to slightly move when no one was looking. Sometimes it looked like they moved closer and other times they had moved further away. Some people even claimed to see the dummies waving at people who drove by beckoning a visitor to come up in the yard. While getting candy, trick-or-treaters often asked Dolores about the dummies and how they moved.

"Those dummies don't move. Poke them if you like, but they are just made of old newspapers and rags. They won't get you now but misbehave and they WILL

GET YOU," said Dolores as she clawed at the children in a playful grasping motion, who jumped and giggled.

When Dolores' husband passed away the Halloween House just wasn't same. Dolores would still pass out candy and decorate as much as she could, but the decorations and candy grew thinner with each passing year until she also passed away.

The elderly couple's home was gradually emptied by their surviving family, and the house was put on the market. A "For Sale" sign was stuck in the front yard for some time until it eventually just disappeared. The neighbors simply assumed the family had taken it off the market.

The following Halloween neighbors and trick-or-treaters waited to see if the house would be ready for the holiday. They walked and drove by every day leading up to October 31, but no decorations were set out. It was disheartening to see the local neighborhood attraction unadorned with Halloween decorations.

Halloween had come and trick-or-treaters and parents put on their costumes and fall attire to make the door-to-door trek for candy in other neighborhoods that still participated in the holiday. People still drove by the Halloween House with their kids hoping to see any sign of activity coming from the home, but there was none. All they could do was reminisce about how it used to be. The old Halloween House sat silent and dark as the sun set and street lights popped on.

However, something eerily strange happened that particular Halloween evening. As the sun disappeared behind the horizon the Halloween House's porch light flickered on! Neighbors passing by pulled over or stopped walking down the street when they saw the porch light. Then they saw what appeared to be the vague appearance of a dummy standing in the shadows of the side yard waving. Trick-or-treaters darted up the front yard and approached the dummy to get a better glimpse of it but as they drew closer it disappeared into the shadows of the side yard. This still delighted the kids since the dummies had been known to do that before.

"Surely they are handing out candy," thought everyone who had seen the waving dummy!

The trick-or-treaters ran back around to the front of the house and up the stairs to the front door. They knocked, but no one came to answer. They rang the doorbell, but no bells or chimes could be heard echoing inside. The trick-or-treaters waited a while longer. They looked back at their parents, but their parents just shrugged their shoulders. They had all seen the dummy waving and the porch light was still on, but no one came out to give them candy. The children and their parents casually backed away, confused. Some people tried to peer through the windows, but all they could see was a dark empty house. Others ventured back to the side yard to look for the waving dummy, but the dummy was unable to be found.

To this day they Halloween House still exists. Older now, it has fallen into disrepair and yard is overgrown, much like the neighborhood around it. No one appears to be living in it; however, it is said you can still drive down the road on Halloween night and see its porch light flickering on and off. And if you peer hard enough and long enough into the dark side yard of the house, perhaps you will see one of the old couple's Halloween dummies in the shadows waving at you. I do.

Old Boy

Ricky's house was on a corner which saw some of the busiest traffic in the neighborhood. He watched all sorts of automobiles putt up and down Main Street which ran parallel with the right side of the house and intersected with 3rd Street out in the front. Kids came and went on the sidewalks as they left for school in the morning and returned in the afternoon to play.

It was an old home in an old neighborhood. The houses had been built close together and painted with tasteful traditional colors, but for as long as Ricky could remember he was mesmerized by the sounds and colors of cars and trucks whizzing in all directions at the intersection of 3rd and Main.

His parents told him how Main Street had once been a trail the pioneers traversed. On the other side of Main Street was the south end of old downtown. During the turn of the century, trolley cars would clang and clatter up and down the street. When the neighborhood was plotted, people requested that the trolley not come so far south because traffic made it difficult for people to walk to work and for children going to school. The neighborhood's request to move the trolley route was eventually granted when too many accidents began accumulating at the intersection of 3rd and Main.

Tony and Albert were Ricky's best friends. They often came over to play board games, share comics, or hang out in Ricky's clubhouse and play with the toy cars in which Ricky had a fascination. Ricky's interest with cars came from watching his father who was a mechanic and sometimes brought home other people's cars on which to work.

Ricky, also, enjoyed being outside. When the weather was nice, he spent a lot of time on the front porch of his house, and the whole neighborhood was his playground; however, he could not say the same for his house.

Ricky's house had always unnerved him. His parents never noticed anything out of the norm, but Ricky did. He often saw creeping shadows out of the corners of his eyes and heard strange noises like something was howling or growling. Ricky used to complain to his parents, but they always explained to him that it was just the house settling or the lights from cars going by causing the strange shadows he was seeing. On top of the shadows and eerie sounds of the house, strange balls would sometimes show up in the house. Tennis balls, baseballs, golf balls, and even the occasional football would find their way into the home. They didn't have any pets, so according to

Ricky's parents attributed all the balls to Ricky and his friends.

Ricky stayed outside as much as he could in order to avoid the strange occurrences in the house, but he couldn't avoid bedtime and sleep. Going to bed in the house was challenging at times. Outside lights *could* cast weird shadows which could make one think that someone was standing behind them or crawling on the floor toward them. It didn't help that Ricky had read one too many comic books about ghosts, goblins, demons, and monsters, and his imagination ran wild at the idea of something haunting the house.

Once Ricky was under his covers and his parents settled in for the night the noises seemed to grow louder and larger as he fell asleep. These strange things didn't happen all the time, but when they did Ricky had to tell himself that what he was seeing and hearing wasn't real. Over time he simply ignored it all and thought about the things he like in order to help him fall asleep. He was able to do this until the night of his thirteenth birthday.

Ricky brushed his teeth, as he did every night, before hopping into bed. The night was like any other except for the anticipation of his birthday in the morning. He tucked himself in and wondered about what presents he might receive as he gradually fell asleep.

It was just past midnight when Ricky woke up. He'd had a nightmare that frightened him out of his sleep, and his heart was beating fast. He needed to calm down, so he got up and lumbered to the bathroom across the hall to get a drink of water. As he shuffled along, he tried recalling his nightmare. Images of a four legged beast flickered in his head. It was watching him from the shadows of his house, but he couldn't get a clear view of what it was. The beast crawled from shadow to shadow, looking at him with bright bluish-green eyes.

Ricky turned on the bathroom light, drank from the faucet, and splashed his face to cool down. He remembered more from the nightmare when the cold water hit his face. This beast made growling and howling noises just like the house had always made. When the beast took a step toward Ricky in his nightmare that is when he jerked awake. He clutched his chest and took a few deep breathes telling himself that it was just a dream.

Ricky was able to relax a little after splashing his face and decided to head back to bed. As he turned off the bathroom light and stepped into the hallway, he was startled by the sound of a chilling howl coming from the end of the hallway near the top of the staircase. Ricky's blood pulsed rapidly as he turned in the direction of the howl. There at the end of the hallway at the top of the stairs were two large bluish-green eyes glowing back at him! The eyes were surrounded by a hairy black mass suspended in the air by four long legs. Ricky slumped against the wall as he tried to scream, but couldn't and collapsed to the floor.

His parents heard the commotion of Ricky falling in the hallway and rushed to his side. When they turned on the hallway light the four legged beast disappeared from Ricky's sight. He tried to tell his parents something had been near the top of the stairs, but his panic made it difficult for his parents to understand what he was saying. Ricky passed out and when he awoke he was back in his bed with his parents were standing over him.

Ricky's parents were relieved to see him awake and they had a flurry of questions for him. He answered them, but quickly cut them off and asked them about the wild animal in the house. His parents looked at him, perplexed, as he told them about his dream and then seeing this creature in the hallway. His parents told him it was just his mind playing tricks on him and the comic books he read probably contributed to it. They assured him that it was probably just a hallucination from quickly awakening from a deep sleep.

Ricky was disappointed that his parents didn't believe him. He began to doubt himself about what he had seen and thought, perhaps, he did imagine it all.

The next day his father and mother went about their business as usual, but Ricky was still on edge. He stared at the top of the stairs from the living room floor. Feeling anxious, he promptly stepped outside the house to calm his nerves. Ricky sat on the front porch swing and gently rocked while contemplating the previous night's events. Ricky worried about going to bed; he neither wanted to dream of this thing again, nor see it if he were to awake during the middle of the night.

Ricky's worries turned to relief when his friends, Tony and Albert, shouted for him from down the street. They sprinted down to the sidewalk and dashed up the yard to Ricky's side to wish him a happy birthday, but they noticed his pallid demeanor and asked what was wrong. When Ricky's parents were nowhere in sight, he leaned in close to Tony and Albert and told them what had happened to him in the middle of the night. He described his dream, then told them about waking up to see the hairy beast in the hall and hearing it make the same noises the house had always made.

Tony and Albert were completely fascinated, although somewhat terrified, by what Ricky described seeing and hearing. Ricky was relieved that his friends, at least, listened to him. They believed him more than his parents.

Albert was particularly captivated by Ricky's experience. He'd read a lot of monster comic books, too, and Ricky's story definitely sounded like one of those. Albert asked about the noises in the house and wanted Ricky to imitate them. Ricky mimicked them to the best of his ability and that really piqued Albert's interest.

Suddenly, Ricky had an idea. Ricky knew he was going to have trouble sleeping that night and Albert wanted to hear the noises, so since it was a Friday night and it was his birthday it was a perfect night for a sleep over! He ran the idea past Tony and Albert and they were completely up for staying the night.

Ricky went inside to ask his parents who were reluctant at first given the events of the previous night, but eventually approved since it was his birthday. Tony and Albert rushed home to get approval from their parents who gave them the okay, and they quickly gathered up their stuff for the sleep over. They even packed a few things that they thought could possibly capture Ricky's creature.

They all met later that afternoon in Ricky's backyard clubhouse where they talked about what they may hear or see that night. Albert insisted on staying up all night to catch a glimpse of what Ricky had seen. He brought his parent's camera along in the hopes of snapping a picture of the four legged beast Ricky had described, and he also brought his parent's old tape recorder to capture the haunting sounds of the house. Tony was going to be the muscle. He was considered fearless by his friends, and was going to stand between his friends and anything that may want to do them harm.

They further discussed the four legged beast over pizza and board games in the clubhouse until an evening storm came in and a chilling wind whistled through the little shack. Ricky's mother shouted from the back door of the house for the boys to come inside. Ricky, Tony, and Albert looked at one another with a bit of hesitancy, but were prepared for the long night ahead.

Since Ricky's parents didn't believe what he had seen and didn't pay attention to the noises the house made, the boys thought it best not to tell his parents about their plan to stay up all night. They entered the house and discreetly glanced around corners as they made their way upstairs. They wanted to avoid any suspicion from Ricky's parents. If they were to find out what the three friends were up to that night, they would surely call off the sleepover.

The boys cautiously marched up the stairs and passed the point where Ricky had seen the four legged creature standing and staring at him. They filed into Ricky's room, quickly closed the door behind them, laid out their sleeping bags, and readied themselves for the night's adventure.

After Ricky's mom came in and wished them goodnight, they sprang into stakeout action. While Ricky pressed his ear against his door and listened until his parents went to bed, Albert began rigging the camera to snap a picture if the door was opened by anyone other than them. When Ricky's parent's bedroom door finally shut, the boys clicked on a lamp and pulled out items to keep them entertained while they waited for the strange events of the house to occur. They stayed up as long as they could, playing games, reading comic books, and talking until one by one they all, gradually, fell asleep.

The storm rolled in and rain had started heavily pelting the house. While the soothing sounds of a summer rain kept the boys conked out, the house began to make its usual eerie noises. A groaning noise was made from just outside room, but the boys only stirred and did not wake. Suddenly, Ricky's bedroom door began to slowly open. Albert's camera rig was tripped and a photo was snapped! The boys, however, didn't hear the snap of the camera or notice its flash in the midst of the storm flashing and splashing outside.

The door opened halfway and unseen footsteps were making their way toward Ricky's bed. Then, Ricky's bed began to sink, as if a great weight was standing upon it.

Ricky awoke and was stunned with a paralyzing fear. Looking him directly in the face were two bluish-green eyes surrounded by a large black mass of hair supported by four long legs. It was the beast! Ricky could feel its heavy breath fogging his face and his heart raced, thinking he was about to be eaten. The beast's mouth opened and Ricky was powerless to give a shout. Just when he thought the thing was going to sink his teeth into his face, a large tongue swept passed its snarling fangs and began licking his cheek.

Instantly, Ricky's fear turned to confusion. Then a click sounded in the room. The beast looked up and spotted Albert who had awakened. The paralyzing effect lifted and Ricky was able to whisper Albert's name. Albert clicked on a flashlight and saw Ricky with eyes wide open and staring directly at him. Albert was shocked with fright when he saw the two bluish green eyes with Ricky staring at him, too! He rubbed his own eyes and when he opened them again, only Ricky was staring at him. The beast had vanished!

Albert looked at Ricky, and just as he was about to ask if that was the creature, Ricky nodded his head yes.

Albert said, "I got it!"

Trembling, Ricky sputtered, "You got what?"

Albert turned his flashlight to the tape recorder. The click that had drawn the attention of the beast was Albert's tape recorder stopping after the tape had run out. He had pressed the record button earlier when he started nodding off.

Tony finally woke up when he heard his friends talking. They told Tony what happened and were all fully awake, unable to go back to sleep. They did not want to listen to the recording until the sun was up, but Albert did pick up the instant photo that was snapped by the camera. He couldn't believe his eyes! He stood silent with his mouth, gaping in horror. He handed the photo to Ricky and Tony, and they gasped at what was captured. In the photo, the door was half open and two bluish green eyes peered in from the hallway surrounded by a black hairy mass and four long legs!

After the boys terrifying sleepover experience at Ricky's house, they met up later that day at the clubhouse to go over what had happened. Albert brought the tape recorder with him. They feared playing the tape because of what they might hear, but Tony went ahead and pressed the play button while Ricky and Albert hesitated. The old player began to turn the tape and white noise along with the cascade of rain crept through the speaker. They listened for a half hour and nothing was heard until Ricky picked up on a familiar noise.

"There!" said Ricky. He rewound the tape so the other two could hear it. It was faint, but Tony and Albert listened closely and heard a distant groaning noise, as if someone was expressing discomfort.

"There is no way that could be the house!" said Albert. "Houses creak, crack, and knock, but this was something groaning!"

They continued to listen closely for a while longer until, eventually, another groan was made, followed by what sounded like a growling animal. This time it was clearer and sounded closer to the recorder. The tape was nearing the end when the last sounds came forth. The slight squeak of Ricky's bedroom door was heard opening. Footsteps that sounded like sharp claws tapped the floor with every step. The boys nearly jumped when a low growl rumbled through the speaker. Whatever it was, it came close to the tape recorder. Heavy breathing and sniffing could be heard, as if some creature was curious of the tape recorder.

Finally, they heard the sound of compressing bed springs, as if something large and heavy had sat itself on top the bed. A deep billowing growl descended into the white noise of the recorder and then the player clicked off.

To the boys, the answers were clear. Ricky's house was haunted by a strange beast that must come out at night!

Ricky dreaded the following evening. When bedtime came that night he didn't know what to do. His parents wouldn't believe that this thing could open doors and that it only came around when he was asleep. Ricky purposely dilly-dallied when his parents told him to go to bed. Unfortunately, he could not hold up his ruse for very long, and his parents' patience ran out. Up to bed he went, dragging all the way. He slowly brushed his teeth and when he was finished, he darted across the hallway hoping to not encounter the creature on his way to his room. Ricky jumped into bed and drew the sheets over his head, leaving just a big enough gap in his covers for air. He trembled with fright knowing something not of this world was in the house. He couldn't think of anything happy to ease his thoughts but finally succumbed to the protective comfortable blankets and fell asleep, still afraid.

Later that night while Ricky deeply slept, the eerie noises began once again. His bedroom door slowly opened and a low groan billowed in the room. Claws on the hardwood floor tapped with every step, but Ricky didn't wake up. The steps stopped at the edge of Ricky's bed. Another low groan next to Ricky's bed was made, but he still didn't wake up. Then something plopped on the bed, and Ricky sprang awake and wildly looked around.

He looked at his partially, opened bedroom door and shuddered, but he didn't see the creature around his bed. He looked down in his lap, and nestled in the sheets was a red ball but unlike one that he had ever seen before. Confused, Ricky picked up the ball and examined it, then it hit him. He flung the ball from his sight and it bounced through the bedroom doorway and out into the hall. Ricky grabbed his covers and pulled them back over his head. Before he could even think of trying to go back to sleep he heard his bedroom door creak open further. Ricky slowly sat up and peeled his bed covers down to just his nose. Then he saw it! In the doorway there were two bluish-green eyes staring back at him. Before Ricky could shriek, he noticed something round and red just below the glowing eyes.

"The ball!" Ricky said aloud.

When Ricky spoke the beast stepped back into the room filling Ricky with fear as it came around the bed with its claws tapping along the way. Ricky was able to see the beast more clearly as it walked into the dim street light that shone in from the window.

Ricky's fear slightly eased when the beast took on a less fearsome appearance. The hairy black mass appeared to just be messy fur. Its claws were long, but dull, and the glowing eyes now had a face to go with it. The beast's terrifying form lessened, and Ricky could now see that this was no monster, it was just a dog! It was an old looking dog that hadn't been groomed in some time.

Its face was not vicious or snarling. It was kind, and expressed the playful enthusiasm of a puppy with a toy. Ricky was surprised to find himself calming down in the presence of this strange old dog. The dog's eyes still glowed, but with a gentle gaze as it stared at Ricky. It took a few steps closer to edge of Ricky's bed and plopped the ball down on his covers once again. Ricky looked at the ball and realized the real reason behind all the mysterious balls that showed up in the house! Ricky slowly picked up the ball while not breaking his gaze with the dog and said, "You just want to play don't you, old boy?"

The dog's tail rose from behind it and began to wag eagerly from side to side. Ricky tossed the ball into the corner of the room and the dog swiftly pounced upon it. Ricky's fear turned to delight as he watched the dog waddle back over and plop the ball on back onto the bed. Ricky grinned from ear to ear as he tossed the ball again and the old dog retrieved it.

Just as he was about to throw the ball again his ceiling light flipped on and his mother stood in the doorway glowering at Ricky and said with a stern whisper, "Ricky! It is way past your bedtime! Put that ball away and go to sleep!"

Ricky looked at his mom and then looked back to the dog, but the dog had vanished. He looked at his mom with a stunned expression, and with a little bit of clarity he had just nodded his head up and down. His mother just stared back at him, then snapped the light switch off and stormed back to bed.

Ricky remained sitting up looking around the room for the dog, but it was nowhere in sight. Ricky laid back down listening for any noise that could be the dog coming back, but no unusual sound was heard. While pondering where it could have possibly gone, he slipped back to sleep.

The next day Ricky was playing in the backyard and thinking about the creature that came to visit him at night. "What was he? Is he a ghost? Where did he go? Where does he come from?"

Then something caught his attention out the corner of his eye, and he spotted a red ball rolling out from the back bushes of his yard. Ricky looked beyond the red ball and into the bushes. Staring out from the shade of the leaves were two familiar bluish-green eyes staring back at him!

With a mix of shock and wonder, he found himself captivated by this thing's gaze. Ricky's curiosity made him want to see if the dog would come closer to him. He looked around to see if anyone else was nearby, but no one was walking on Main Street and no one was lingering on the other side of his house since the house next door was up for sale.

Ricky whistled and said, "Hey, come here."

The dog gazed on and let out a low groan. Ricky repeated himself, and to his astonishment, the dog took a few steps out of the bushes.

"That's it old boy!" said Ricky, looking on in wonder.

The old dog waddled out a little further and was able to seen with sunlight shining on its back. Ricky coaxed the dog out a little further, until it was, almost, in petting distance.

"Come on old boy, that's it!" exclaimed Ricky.

After another tentative step, Ricky reached out and try to pet the strange beast and the dog stretched its nose to his hand. Ricky felt its breath tickle his fingertips. He reached further and his hand gently patted the dog's head. To his surprise, it felt like a real dog. The dog was dirty and desperately needed a brush. Mud was caked in its fur and only bones could be felt under its matted hair. For a moment Ricky believed him to be real and looked around to see if anyone was watching, but still no one was nearby.

"You're not scary at all, you're a good old boy aren't you?" said Ricky as he continued patting and petting him on the head while looking him over. The dog didn't have a collar and Ricky couldn't tell what breed it was or even the exact color of its fur. He just looked like an old and dirty dog.

"I wonder what your name is. How about for now I just call you Old Boy? Seems fitting for you and you do respond to it. Old Boy, it is! My name is Ricky, can you shake?" asked Ricky as he extended his other hand. To Ricky's amazement, Old Boy lifted his paw and landed right in Ricky's hand. Ricky laughed out loud!

"You need to meet my friends, Tony and Albert, officially this time and not in such a creepy manner during the night. Stay right here, I'll be right back!" said Ricky as he slowly walked away from Old Boy who remained sitting where Ricky had been playing.

Ricky dashed over to Tony's and Albert's house and told them they had to come over right away to meet his new friend. With Tony's and Albert's parents nearby, Ricky spoke to them privately, so as not to startle the adults.

While Tony and Albert got ready to go to Ricky's house, Ricky ran back to his backyard to see Old Boy, but he was gone. Ricky whistled and shouted for him, and then he heard a commotion in his clubhouse. Ricky ran over to clubhouse and swung open the door. He laughed when he saw Old Boy rummaging through a storage box that had some of Ricky's toys in it. The dog turned around with a yellow, squeaky ball in his mouth. Ricky just smiled said, "Of course, you would pick a ball out of there."

After a few minutes Tony and Ricky came bolting through the clubhouse door and saw Ricky propping up a large board.

"Where is he?! Is he here?!" asked Tony and Albert. Ricky's friends rapidly threw out more questions until he calmed them down.

"He is here," said Ricky. "Now, don't freak out. He is actually kind of skittish."

Tony cocked his head back and said, "I don't ever freak out. I'm ready."

Albert just nodded and looked on bracing himself.

"I don't know what you guys will think, but tell me what you see when I move this board out of the way," said Ricky as he looked behind the board with a smirk.

Ricky stepped to one side and scooted the board away. Albert's jaw dropped and Tony shrieked and fled the clubhouse in horror! They saw a ball floating in mid-air for a few seconds until it dropped to the floor and rolled to Tony's feet.

When Albert and Ricky finally coaxed "tough guy" Tony back into the clubhouse, they got a better chance to meet Old Boy after they recovered from the shock of seeing something unbelievable. Tony had described to Ricky and Albert seeing only a floating ball, but Albert saw what he thought was a dog holding a ball in its mouth.

"Precisely!" exclaimed Ricky. Before they could get to know Old Boy better, the boys became distracted by the sound of screeching brakes out near the front of Ricky's house.

The boy's attention was drawn to a large moving truck pulling up to the house for sale next to Ricky's. The boys peered out of the clubhouse window and saw the back door of the house next to Ricky's swing open. A man and woman stepped out followed by a young girl in a pink dress and a younger girl in a blue dress. The girls ran with joy to the swing set left by the previous owners. The youngest girl looked to be just a baby learning to walk, but the older girl looked to be about the same age as Ricky, Albert, and Tony. The woman noticed the boys looking their way. She leaned over to the older girl with a smile and whispered to her. The girl looked up and over from the swing, smiled, and blushed. The woman gently nudged her from the swing set and the girl walked over to the fence next to Ricky's house, with a bit of embarrassment.

"Hi," said the girl to the boys who were, awkwardly, staring at her from the clubhouse windows. Her sandy blonde hair was pulled back with a bow, her brilliant blue eyes sparkled, and her dimpled smile beamed in the summer sun. To the boys she was prettiest girl they had ever seen, but they would never admit it aloud.

After awkwardly staring at her too long, Ricky finally shook his head and responded, "Hi. I'm Ricky and this is Tony and Albert."

The girl's dimple deepened when she replied with her name. "My name is Stacy and I'm your new neighbor!"

From that day on, Stacy would become good friends with Ricky, Tony, and Albert. The boys liked her and didn't want to scare her off by introducing her to Old Boy right away. They kept him secret for a while until she began to get curious about this mysterious friend the boys would sometimes mention.

One day Stacy's curiosity got the best of her. On her way to meet up with the boys, she snuck over to Ricky's clubhouse where the boys were hanging out. She peeked through a crack in the wall of the clubhouse and gasped out loud when she saw the boys sitting around a table watching and laughing at a yellow ball that was floating in mid-air. The boys became alarmed at the subtle noise she made outside the clubhouse. They quickly rushed to see Stacy crouched down and looking up at them with a concerned look on her face. She asked them, "What was holding up that ball?"

The boys looked at one another and wondered if they should finally tell her about their mystery friend. Ricky took her hand, pulled her up, and asked her if she could keep a promise. Stacy stared at Ricky with a bit of bewilderment, but told him that she could keep a promise. Ricky told her if he introduced her to their mystery friend that she could not tell anyone else, not even her parents. Stacy looked at Ricky's hand holding hers and then she looked back up at his eyes. She felt her heart flutter at the excitement of meeting the boy's mystery friend and the genuine look of care in Ricky's eyes gazing back at her. She nodded her head, yes, and told Ricky that she promised to keep this a secret.

Ricky and the boys led her inside the clubhouse where they stood around a table while Stacy looked on with anticipation. Her eyes searched the room for the floating ball but didn't see it.

"You may want to sit down for this," said Tony as he slid a box over for her to sit.

Ricky picked up the ball from behind the table and said, "This may looked spooky at first, but I promise you there is nothing to be afraid of."

Ricky held the ball out to his side. Slowly, he began to take his fingers off the ball one by one until it remained floating in the air. Stacy held her hands over her mouth and her eyes widened, fixed on the floating ball.

"How? What...?" uttered Stacy through her fingers.

"Stacy, meet Old Boy. Old Boy, this is Stacy. Don't worry, she is nice and a friend," Ricky said as he looked down at his side with a smile. Ricky went on to explain how Old Boy came about. Stacy was still in disbelief as she listened to his story and watched the ball float around.

"Would you like to pet him?" asked Ricky.

At first Stacy hesitated, but with Tony and Albert's assurance she worked up the courage to extend her hand over the floating ball. She waved her hand from side to side, looking for strings or anything holding the ball up, but there was nothing there. Ricky gently grabbed her wrist and pulled her hand closer.

"Lower your hand just a few inches and you will be patting Old Boy on the head," said Ricky.

Her fear succumbed to curiosity. She lowered her hand and felt the strangest sensation in her fingertips. The air was cooler and her hand tingled as if it were being vibrated. She smiled with delight, like Ricky first did when he knew that Old Boy wasn't bad.

"Can you guys see him?" asked Stacy.

Albert spoke up. "Ricky can see him and I can sometimes see him, but Tony can't see him at all. However, we can all feel him."

They all smiled and had a good laugh as they all petted and played with Old Boy.

Over the next few years their friendships had grown, but, also had grown apart. Tony's parents had moved away and Tony had to go with them. Albert was accepted into a private high school and spent more time studying than he did playing, but he did still find time to hang out with Ricky and Stacy when he could. As for Ricky and Stacy, they grew closer as they progressed through the same high school together. Having the same classes led to studying, studying led to *going steady*, and going steady led to long walks home from school and late night trips to the rive-in together. Ricky and Stacy had fallen in love with one another. They made plans to finish high school, attend the same college, find a place of their own, and spend the rest of their lives together. However, they didn't know what to do with Old Boy.

Old Boy never left Ricky's house or yard. Ricky and Old Boy had become the best of friends through the years, and Ricky didn't know what would happened to him if he were to move away. Boy and dog comforted each other and had a genuine friendship. Ricky shared all his cares and concerns with Old Boy and Old Boy was always there at his side to listen. Ricky could tell that the dog loved him and loved it when he was around. The idea of leaving Old Boy devastated Ricky, but he knew the time was coming when life would change and he would have to move away.

Stacy knew this too, but her connection to Old Boy was not as strong as Ricky's. At times, Stacy felt that Ricky cared more for Old Boy than he did for her, but that was not the case. Ricky loved Stacy emotionally and romantically, and he loved Old boy as if he were a brother or a child. However, disagreement was inevitable as it is in all relationships. One day Ricky and Stacy had an argument about their future and the day changed their lives forever.

It had been raining all day, and Albert had stopped by to hang out with Ricky. They drank pops on Ricky's front porch and reminisced about their younger days. Albert reminded Ricky that it was a day like that one when he had first told them about Old Boy. They laughed about how scared they were that first stormy night when Old Boy crept into Ricky's room. Albert asked Ricky where Old Boy was and Ricky chuckled because he told him that Old Boy was sitting right next him. Albert smiled reached over and felt around for him. Sure enough he felt the cool and tingly air of

Old Boy. For a few seconds Albert could see the dog's happy panting face staring up at him. Then Albert asked where Stacy was. Just then, they heard the screen door squeak open then slammed shut next door.

"Still having a disagreement I take it?" asked Albert. Ricky just smirked.

Stacy stormed over and planted herself at the bottom of the porch stairs. "Hi Albert. Ricky? We need to talk!"

"Stacy, Albert is over here, you know we don't get to see each other that often," said Ricky. "Come up out of the rain and visit awhile."

"This is important Ricky and I'm sorry Albert but I have to talk with Ricky in private," said Stacy sternly.

"Hey it's cool. I'll just-" Ricky cut him off.

"No Albert, you just stay here," said Ricky.

His tone upset Stacy and she stormed off to the sidewalk and stood in the rain. Ricky shouted for her to come back, but Stacy proceeded to sit on the street curb.

"I guess I better go talk with her," said Ricky to Albert and Old Boy with another smirk.

As he made his way out to Stacy, he heard the screen door slam shut again. Stacy's younger sister, Rosie, had come outside wearing her rain boots and jacket. She hopped on her tricycle and rode down the driveway and then to the sidewalk.

Albert finished his drink on Ricky's porch and told Old Boy that he would just come back later. He set down his drink, waved at Old Boy, wherever he was, and made his way back to his house.

"Come on Stacy. Albert is leaving and your commotion is drawing your sister's attention. Let's get out of the rain and talk," said Ricky with more concern.

"So now I'm making a commotion?" snapped Stacy as she got up and started walking further down the sidewalk.

She began laying into Ricky about the argument and Ricky argued back. Old Boy sat up from the front porch and began barking. They walked farther down the sidewalk until it ended at the intersection. Stacy and Ricky shouted at one another as they continued to cross the intersection. Old Boy began to bark louder as Ricky and Stacy now stood on the other side of Main Street. They continued arguing with one another, but Ricky was becoming frustrated because he couldn't pay attention to what Stacy was saying Old Boy's incessant loud barking.

"Stop barking!" Ricky turned and shouted at Old Boy.

When he did this he saw Rosie crossing the intersection just as a dump truck was speeding down Main Street.

The sound of screeching tires and crunching metal echoed throughout the neighborhood. Albert was several houses down when he heard the crash, but he immediately turned around and took off running back to Ricky's house. Stacy shrieked in horror, as she watched her little sister's tricycle tumble up Main Street. Ricky's parents, Stacy's parents, and the rest of the neighbors came rushing out of their homes and gathered at the intersection. Some held each other while others tended to the body.

Albert arrived, pushing people aside, fearing what he might see, but needing to know what happened. When he had a clear view, Albert began to weep. Stacy was on her knees sobbing and clutching the lifeless body. The front end of the dump truck was caved in and the tricycle down the road was twisted beyond recognition. Albert turned to his side and saw Stacy's sister being comforted by her mother.

Albert listened in on what the neighbors were saying. "I saw it from the window. I heard them shouting at one another then he turned around and dove in front of the truck to push the little girl out of the way! Ricky saved her life."

Stacy pleaded for Ricky to wake up. Tears poured from her face on to his. Suddenly, she heard Ricky draw a breath His eyes opened and he looked up at Stacy. Through her tears, she told him that he saved her sister's life.

Ricky stopped her and whispered, "It was Old Boy. He saved her."

Stacy looked at him and said with a tearful smile, "That's why you said, 'Stop barking.' I thought you were saying that to me."

Ricky snickered as blood trickled down his cheek and his eyes rolled back as he did.

"You are going to be okay, Ricky. The ambulance is on its way. Stay with me, Ricky!" Stacy pleaded as she stroked his cheek.

Ricky parents knelt by their son's side. His mother held his hand and begged him to stay with them.

Ricky turned to them and said, "The sun is out. It feels so warm."

Ricky's parents looked up and said, "Ricky, it is still raining."

Ricky's eyes wandered around until they became fixed on something. He cracked a smile and said "Old Boy."

Ricky's parents asked him what "Old Boy" meant, but he didn't say. They looked at Stacy to see if she could offer an explanation, but she just looked back down at Ricky with her tear-filled eyes. Ricky spoke again, but his words were fading into breathy whispers.

"The day turned out to be so bright and beautiful. Look at Old Boy, he looks great. He looks younger and he is not dirty anymore." Ricky turned his eyes back toward the sky as if he'd heard something. Ricky's gaze shifted from the sky to his feet.

"Okay," he said as his head slighted nodded up and down.

"Okay what? Yes, you will be okay!" said Stacy. But she was unsure to what he was saying okay.

Ricky coughed as he tried to speak again, but the only words he said were, "I love you all. I have to go now. Old Boy and I are going for a walk. I love you all."

Then Ricky closed his eyes and passed to a better life with his love, his family, and a best friend at his side.

Albert bowed his head down as he watched his best friend pass away before his eyes. His tears poured heavier than the rain. He collapsed to the curb and put his hands over his head and then his head to his knees, distraught that his friend was gone. Albert didn't have many friends and none were as good to him as Ricky.

As Albert sat on the curb with a hurting heart, he suddenly felt a hand touch him on the shoulder. He looked up from his knees and couldn't believe what he saw. Ricky was standing over him and Old Boy was at his side!

Before he could exclaim Ricky's name in delight, he saw Ricky hold his finger to his lips to hush Albert. Then Ricky pointed back to where his body was. His body was still there being wept over by Ricky's parents and Stacy. Albert looked around to see if anyone else noticed him, but no one paid any attention to what *he* was seeing. Albert looked back up at Ricky who had that smirk on his face for which he was well known. Old Boy walked over to Albert and licked his face. Albert felt the sensation of a rain drop and tears being whisked away from his cheek.

Ricky knelt down to Albert, placed both of his hands on Albert's shoulder, and then pressed his forehead to Albert's forehead. Albert felt comforted in a strange way. He could see that Ricky was okay and that he was with Old Boy who was okay, too. Ricky stood up and looked down at Old Boy, then looked behind him as did the dog. Albert peered around them to see what they were looking at. He saw a bright light shining from some unknown source, and that is when Albert put it together and he understood that Ricky and Old Boy had to go.

Albert watched Ricky walked over to his parents and Stacy and placed his hands on them in comfort. Ricky then turned his attention back to Albert who was watching this unbelievable sight with a slight smile and teary eyes. Albert saw Ricky's lips move and motion to Old Boy who was still at Albert's side. Ricky whistled for Old Boy to follow him, and the dog gave one more lick to Albert's face then walked over to Ricky's side.

Ricky smiled at Albert and raised his hand to wave goodbye. Albert also raised his hand slightly to wave to Ricky and Old Boy. Ricky placed his hand over his heart and spoke to Albert. He couldn't hear him, but he somehow knew what he said.

"I'll be here," said Ricky motioning to his heart.

Then Ricky turned around and started walking toward the bright light with Old Boy following at his side. Albert's heart was broken, but it was already healing as he watched his two friends disappear into the fading light.

The sound of the ambulance on its way whirled nearby. Albert rose from the curb and made his way to the back of the crowd. He could hear Stacy being reluctantly pulled away from Ricky's body. The sound of the paramedics rushing to Ricky's aid saddened Albert. They worked to revive him, but Albert knew he was no longer there. Albert stuck his hands in his pockets and lowered his head as he walked away from the accident. He thought about his last few moments with his friends. He would miss them dearly.

Albert's reminiscing was interrupted by a collective gasp heard back at the crash site. Suddenly, Albert heard Stacy joyfully shouting Ricky's name. Albert dashed back as fast as he could. He quickly slipped through the crowd and saw Stacy rejoicing with her hands clasped together.

"He's alive, he's alive!" yelled Stacy when she saw Albert looking on. Albert rushed to Ricky's side and saw the best smirk Ricky had ever shown. Ricky reached for Albert and pulled him close.

Ricky whispered to him, "Old Boy has a new home."

Then Ricky looked up at the parting clouds. There in the sky was the warm sun shining down on them.

Ricky winked at Albert and said, "He is chasing *that* yellow ball now."

This story is dedicated to my dog, Chief. I have never known another living creature to have more spirit than he. Chief has taught me to pay attention to everyone and to go after things that I like in life. The joy he shows me every day when I come home from being away has taught me to love regardless of how my day had gone. It would be a shame to say that animals don't have souls when they have more love and compassion than any one of us. It is foolish to think that I would never see him again when one of us passes away. I know and feel in my heart that we will be friends forever in this life and in the next. I love you, Chief, my old boy.

GHOSTLY POETRY

Haunting verses and rhymes, perfect for spooky times.

This Lonely Road

This lonely road appears to stretch on and on.
We're supposed to camp at dusk and march at dawn.
But the sun has yet to set far in the west.
So I trudge on loyally before I rest.
The further I press on the trees seem to grow.
It feels like the winds of time have ceased to flow.
I often think about lying in tall grass,
dodging bullets and balls from cannons of brass.
Many men charged with weapons as my friends flee.
I must have hid well for they did not see me.
When all of the shots and shouts had gone silent,
I peeked through the grass and saw nothing violent.
As I stood up, I felt a pain in my side.
Blood soaked my jacket. "I AM HIT," I had cried.
Only my echo replied in the still air.
All had vanished to places I know not where.
I need a doctor for I have wounds to cleanse,
but I must find my company and my friends.
So we can fight to bring this war to an end,
and reunite this country that needs to mend.
Until then I will march with my weapons drawn,
upon this lonely road that is stretching on.

The Ghost Seeker

They will look for a ghost,
where it is haunted most,
or find them in a place,
where they don't leave a trace.
With their names like "hunter,"
and "investigator,"
they speak to empty rooms,
and explore the dead's tombs.
To see ghosts is a treat,
for those who seek to meet.

Sometimes voices are heard,
whispering a soft word.
The psychics can see them,
looking jolly or grim.
The sensitives feel them,
touching with a cold limb.
A skeptic will deny,
when ghosts do not reply,
but fast and far they'll run,
when spirits have their fun.
The brave and courageous,
thrive on the dangerous,
but if they tempt too much,
Death will wait with its touch.

The Legend of Jeannie Belle

The poor went up the mountains and the rich came
    down,
for a while Ouray was the wealthiest town.
The mountain's quarried treasures were a sight to
    behold,
streaming down their sides were nuggets of silver and
    gold,
but when the miner's greed had dug them too deep,
they disturbed an ancient spirit from its sleep.
A ghost leaped forth clad in black except for its face,
which was pale and undistinguishable in race.
It haunted men day and night,
driving them to death in fright.
The precious mined treasures came to a trickle,
as thoughts toward the mountains became fickle.
The town was in distress while the mines went dry,
Until a young woman spoke and started to cry,
"I fear not the mines, nor a ghost,"
said the woman the town knew most.
It was Jeannie Belle, an actress and artist, who was
    new in Ouray.
Boisterous was her opinion and a can-do approach
    was her way.
"Riches await in the mountain cliffs. Give me a pickaxe
    and a chisel,
I will show this great town that a woman can mine
    without any grizzle."
Against the miner's scorning,
she did not heed their warning,
and up into the mountains she went with mining gear
    in tow,
not knowing when she might make it back down to
    Ouray below.

"Beware of the pale faced spirit!" the town folk would
    yell,
as Jeannie Belle disappeared up the old mining trail.
Weeks went by and soon it was a year,
until Jeannie Belle would reappear.
She walked through the door of the Western Hotel,
and went to the bar with a story to tell.
The aroma of perfume and gunpowder had filled the
    bar,
as she staggered in wearily after traveling so far.
Only the bartender had seen her enter,
and she began to talk about her venture.
"The pale faced ghost won't be bothering you again,
he is trapped in a mine that I blew him up in."
"I stole his gold and silver but its weight took a toll,
I was bringing it down but I stumbled in a hole."
"Far I fell, deep down in a well,
walled by cold darkness black as hell."
"I was able to climb my way up and out,
but all my treasure is lost without a doubt."
"Except for what I hold in my hand,
I give it to you, it's worth a grand."
Jeannie Belle watched the door suspiciously,
as she reach over the bar secretly.
She tumbled a large gold nugget to the barkeep
and said, "I am tired now, I think I shall sleep."
The barkeep happily said, "Right away, I'll grab you a
    key,"
but what had happened next he could not understand
    or believe.
He looked down at his guest book to check her into a
    vacant room,
and when he looked up, all that was there was the
    smell of her perfume.
In an instant she was gone from his sight.
Her disappearance gave him such a fright.
He rushed from the bar and gasped, at something
    never seen on the barroom floor.

Painted was the haunting image of Jeannie Belle
    staring at the front door.
Her likeness remains there still on the floor, even to
    this very day.
Check into the Western Hotel to see for yourself in old
    Ouray.

The Mischievous

Their strange shapes and sounds will give you the creeps,
spooking you from shadows or when one sleeps.
With growling and howling and moans and groans,
They will haunt anything from homes to stones.
Some are just lost and looking for some peace,
and others don't want their lives to decease.
Sometimes they're just legs or a grasping arm,
with a floating face not wishing us harm,
and there are those who want to play with us,
known as strange ghosts called the mischievous.

CONCLUSION

Now, you have seen the ghosts of my haunted mind. The stories carry with them the same chills felt the day they were experienced. I hope they delightfully haunt your fascination for ghosts, as they have for me after all these years. Enjoy the book, again and again, with a crackling fire or in the gloom of an overcast day. If you need some company, pick any of these stories to read and you will no longer feel alone. I never felt alone while writing them. If you amuse or scare anyone willing to listen to the stories, then you, too, will be like the ghosts in this book - good, bad, but definitely mischievous.

ABOUT THE AUTHOR

Adam Tillery's interest in ghosts has taken him to many locations where spirits are said to haunt. These paranormal explorations and listening to other people's ghostly experiences inspired him to visually interpret the ghosts he sees in his mind on to paper. The charcoal drawings he has produced with these ghosts have fascinated those who view them due to their close resemblance to spirits and entities seen during paranormal experiences.

Adam has drawn numerous cartoons, comic book heroes, and caricatures of those around him, and he has painted still lifes, portraits, and murals of fantasy landscapes.

Combining his two passions of studying ghosts and creating art has helped ease Adam's need to do more of both. He has captured plenty of voices on audio in empty rooms and seen things move by themselves on video when no one else was around. Ironically, however, he never seen a ghost with his own eyes. Adam believes his gift is not to physically see them, but to feel the spirits around him and put the clues they leave behind together so that he may help them tell their story.

Other titles from Haunted Road Media in which Adam D. Tillery has appeared:

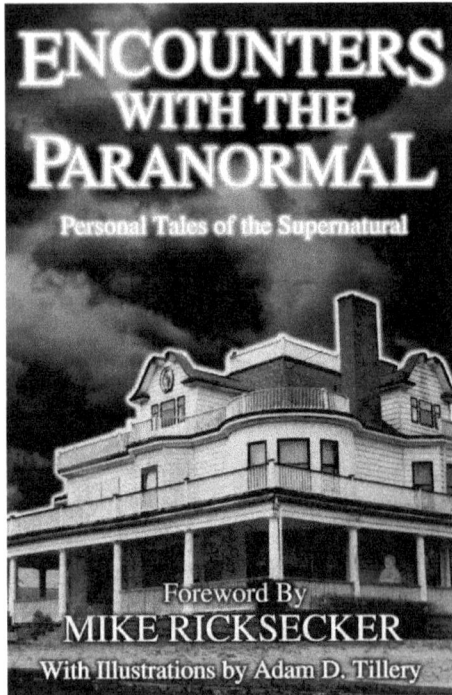

Almost everyone has a ghost story. Real people. Real stories.

Read about haunted houses and vehicles, experiences during paranormal investigations, visits from relatives that have passed on, pets reacting to the paranormal, psychic experiences, and conversations with full-bodied apparitions.

ENCOUNTERS WITH THE PARANORMAL reveals personal stories of the supernatural, exploring the realm beyond the veil through the eyes of a colorful cast of contributors.

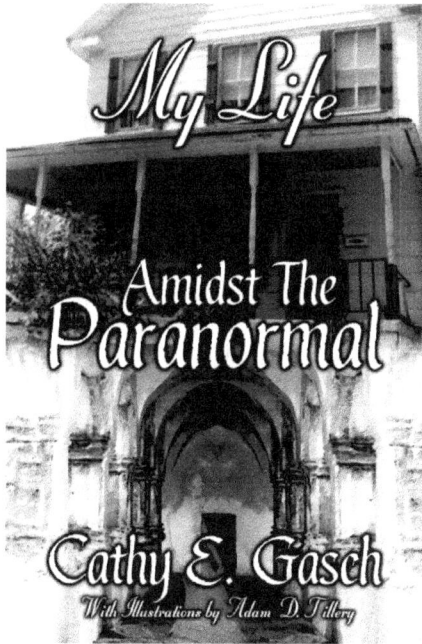

Cathy E. Gasch has been able to sense the paranormal all of her life. Take a journey with her through haunted houses and ancient ruins across three different countries, and discover for yourself what it's like to be sensitive to the paranormal. Mischievous ghosts, spectral apparitions, and forgotten souls abound in this collection of true spooky tales!

With fantastic illustrations by Adam D. Tillery and authentic photographs!

For more information visit:
www.hauntedroadmedia.com

www.ingramcontent.com/pod-product-compliance
Lightning Source LLC
LaVergne TN
LVHW052025080426
835513LV00018B/2171